To our family, friends, and clients who graciously (unwittingly, in some cases) provided us with such rich and wonderful grist for our mill.

Foreward

Martha
and Bobbi

"Friendship is one mind in two bodies."

Mencius

This book evolved in an interesting way, at what must have been just the right time. We've been friends for about twenty years. During that time we've spent many hours walking, meeting for coffee or wine, trading war stories, and simply enjoying each other's company.

We talk a lot about business in general, but skirt around specifics, since we work in the same marketplace and our businesses and clients often overlap. We've always approached the business end of our relationship with respect for each other and our clients' privacy.

Martha *I toyed with the idea of sharing my life and times in a book, but never gained real traction. While walking and thinking one day, I had an "aha" moment: why not bring Bobbi into the project? When I got home, I called her and asked simply, "Do we have a book in us?" The answer was a decisive yes.*

Bobbi *Writing a book had been a dream of mine for a long time but it wasn't yet a priority. It was just a "some day" dream until Martha said it out loud. In that instant it became my goal, my priority, and my passion. I simply had to write down my thoughts and I haven't stopped writing since.*

We began writing "articles" about aspects of our business and our lives we thought might be interesting — second-guessing ourselves every inch of the way. We started emailing them back and forth, and our book took shape. In fact, it seemed to write itself.

At first we thought we should present each topic from our two perspectives. Eventually, we found that more often than not, we shared the same viewpoint — so much so that we were beginning to lose track of who'd written what. The realization slowly dawned on us that we had only one mind between us.

So we played to our strengths and forged ahead. We questioned ourselves daily, shored up each others' confidence as needed, laughed at ourselves, and called for lifelines many times. We used all the techniques we recommend in these pages: We took "baby steps," working on the book just a few minutes each day; we set goals and deadlines; we broke down overwhelming tasks into bite-sized pieces. Clearly, we had fun doing it.

We hope you find a few nuggets in this book to enhance your business and your life. If it does nothing more than help you avoid some of our mistakes, we'll be happy. If knowing we overcame so many blunders gives you the courage to put yourself out there and find true success and happiness, we'd consider our undertaking a huge success.

Acknowledgment

A big thank you to Sally Huss for the perfect cover art and her wonderful Happy Musings sprinkled throughout this book. Sally was the first person we approached when our book was little more than a dream. We only knew her by her work and were astonished and thrilled when she agreed to help us. She was an inspiration to us from the beginning and continues to cheer us on.

Sally Huss, creator of King Features syndicated panel HAPPY MUSINGS, is an illustrator of books, children's books and designer of products from purses to baby bibs. All of her art is happy in nature and free-spirited in style.

To see more art and writings by Sally, including her book *HOW TO GET YOUR MAN – The Slam-Dunk Formula to Getting the Love of Your Life*, go to: www.sallyhuss.com.

table of contents

It's all in your head

But first, the basics

Address your stress

Simple tricks

A new course, and how to chart it

Take it higher

Appendix: Doing the math

1 It's all in your head

If we can do it, so can you

"Believe in yourself! Have faith in your abilities! Without a humble but reasonable confidence in your own powers, you cannot be successful or happy."

— *Norman Vincent Peale*

The two of us are ordinary women — except when it comes to that elusive quality called drive. We are definitely driven. We're organized, and we don't waste time. Other than that, we enjoy a variety of outside activities, are blessed with wonderful families and friends, and, generally speaking, love life. We have our flaws. We've made many mistakes, and

Happy Musings
by Sally Huss
Your potential for greatness is greater than you think.

tried to learn from them. Some are described in embarrassing detail in this book.

We're hoping that with fifty (yikes) combined years in the workplace, having achieved an unusual level of professional success, we just might have something to offer. Our purpose in writing this book is to help you realize your goals by sharing our experiences, and perhaps helping you find an easier path than we sometimes took.

We believe in keeping things simple. We've found it helps us accomplish more. We both still struggle to attain that simplicity — we always seem to have so much going on. But for us, the key is planning and systems.

We met over twenty years ago at a successful local real estate company in Orange County, California. Bobbi was a new agent; Martha was a branch manager whose responsibilities included training new agents.

Bobbi *I remember Martha's style of presenting the necessary professional information while being approachable and funny at the same time. She told the group that while showing property the day before, she'd said to the buyer, "You've seen every outfit I own. It's time to buy a house." Apparently her professional wardrobe was limited in those* *days, and she couldn't bear the thought of repeating. Martha was real then. Fast-forward over two decades, and she still is.*

Martha *From the beginning, I knew Bobbi had what it takes to succeed. She looked and spoke the part, and she certainly wasn't afraid to ask for the order. On signing her first listing, she requested a higher split because she was going to do great things for this company. I believe I reminded her that she had to successfully sell and close a few transactions in order to reap the rewards of a higher split. Nevertheless, I was pretty impressed with this rookie's confidence and poise.*

Through the years, we've been dear friends and fair competitors. We work in the same community, and have competed for desirable listings many times. We have always shared techniques, but never clients' personal information. Over the years, we've met for coffee countless times and even taken golf lessons together (you won't find that on either of our lists of accomplishments). We have always been compatible and shared the same work ethic. We both strive to put our best foot forward, take the high road, live graciously and respect others — and we show up every day ready to work.

Take what resonates with you here and develop your own vision. It really is possible to live your dream. If we can do it, so can you.

The totally outrageous dream

"Dreams are necessary to life."

– Anaïs Nin

What would you do if you knew you could not fail?

Have you always wanted to do what you're doing now? No? Then why are you doing it? What's stopping you from following your dream? Could it be fear of failure?

Do any of these excuses sound familiar? "I'm too old to start something new." "I don't know how to go about it." "It would

Happy Musings
by Sally Huss
Dream big, plan well,
work hard, smile always
and good things
will happen.

take too much effort to start over." "I'm comfortable doing what I know."

What is your passion — that thing that makes you feel energized?

Tell those negative voices to be quiet. Dig deep and breathe slowly. When you're completely immersed in doing or thinking about something and time flies by, what are you doing or thinking about? What have you always wanted to learn to do? What would it feel like to do it?

Did you know that in your psyche, the pull of "comfortable" and "it's not great, but it's okay" is so strong that you'll do something familiar you don't like rather than try something new? Human beings dislike change because it's frightening and uncomfortable. We get used to our jobs, our financial status, our daily routines and our mediocre relationships. We'd rather complain about them than take a chance and change. After all, things could be worse, right?

Ah, but they could be so much better.

Time to stop settling

To change something, you must replace it with something else. If you bite your nails when you're anxious, willpower alone won't change that habit. It needs to be replaced with a new, more positive habit. Maybe chewing gum, or counting to ten, or taking three deep breaths. Repeat the replacement routine enough times, and it becomes the new habit. To change something that isn't working in your life, replace it with something better. Sure, it'll feel odd at first, but keep doing it until it becomes comfortable. Then press on from there.

The first step is to absolutely identify your dream or your passion — that thing that's so charged with emotion that you must see it through — voilá! The next step is to describe it as perfectly and in as much detail as you can. Do this until you can practically see it … it's exciting to think about … and you're intensely committed to achieving it because you love the way you feel when you see yourself there. Now, make tiny goals to get you started on the road to realizing your outrageous dream.

Bobbi *A word of warning: be careful who you share this dream with. Some people may react negatively, because the discussion makes them uncomfortable. Maybe they gave up on their own dreams, or maybe they didn't even try. Find someone who shares your spirit of dreaming big and will cheer you on.*

"Vision without action is merely a dream. Action without vision just passes the time. Vision with action can change the world."

–Joel A. Barker

Zero in on your passion

"Life is to be lived. If you have to support yourself, you had bloody well better find some way that is going to be interesting."

– Katherine Hepburn

Who doesn't love to be around passionate people? They have such wonderfully contagious energy and enthusiasm. A little zest for life goes a long way. You can be one of those people, too. You just need to find your passion and take the time to develop its full potential.

We all have talents and areas of interest. If you have trouble coming up with something that really excites you, revisit your childhood — those delightfully unself-conscious days when you didn't know enough to care what anyone else thought. You know — before you became jaded and stuck in a rut. What piqued your interest back then?

Martha *When I was a kid, I was all girl. I played with dolls and spent countless hours creating fabulous outfits for them. I was a young Martha Stewart. Today, you could* *say I'm an old Martha Stewart. I was also the kid at the breakfast table reading the cereal box from top to bottom. When my grandmother treated me to a cross country train trip in a state-of-the-art dome car with spectacular views of never-ending "amber waves of grain," I didn't see any of them. I had my nose in a book the entire way, much to her disappointment. Today, I belong to two book clubs and always have a few books going. Clearly, my passions haven't changed.*

We spend so much of our time on earth earning a living that it seems a shame to just put in time at a job you don't love. Be passionate about your profession or find another one that lights your fire. Once you've identified it, really go after it. Consider turning your avocation into your vocation.

Sometimes we're just too close to see what's obvious to others. Ask your friends what they think your passion might be. You'll likely get all kinds of opinions, and that's okay. It only takes one to connect with the truth and spark an "ah ha!" moment. We guarantee there's at least one button inside you that lights you up when it's pushed. Play to that strength. Maximize it. Polish it up, and you will shine.

Like it or not, you're a leader

We're all leaders in some way. Our children and our clients look to us for guidance. The world is thirsting for true leadership.

Leaders are expected to be experts in their fields and provide the information and resources people need to make good choices. Your clients, staff, co-workers, and children all want direction and counsel.

When you think about it, the ultimate decisions in real estate are out of your control. As a leader, your job is to guide clients toward those decisions, because people are afraid of making

Happy Musings
by Sally Huss
Every player counts
on a team, no matter
the kind of team!

the wrong choices. Clients look to their agents to boost their confidence — and that requires them to have confidence in your leadership.

We all know charismatic, self-confident people who radiate warmth and fill the room with positive energy. We're drawn to them. What do they have that sets them apart? Leaders are passionate about life. They're solution-oriented, make-it it-happen, non-whiners. They hold themselves and others to a higher standard. They get more because they expect more. They envision people at their full potential instead of where they are now.

Fortunately, leadership qualities can be learned. Self confidence is the touchstone. (Don't confuse confidence with arrogance. All the best leaders have humility and play well with others.)

Eight traits of great leaders

They lead by example. We're not saying that in order to lead, you must live a perfect life. That's simply not going to happen. We're human, and we're all blessed with imperfections. However, good leaders consistently work to improve themselves — and help others in the process.

Martha   I hold sales meetings and training classes every day. I find my message resonates better with agents when it's delivered within a story about myself and a screw-up. It's not that anyone wants to see me fail. Quite the opposite. People like to hear that success is possible despite mistakes. A little fun at my expense helps to illustrate pitfalls to avoid while connecting me to my audience.

They have a sense of fairness. Leaders are good at weighing all sides of an issue to help people reach the most equitable solution possible. "Walk a mile in someone else's shoes" is excellent advice. There are at least two sides to every story, and it helps to get the other person's perspective when you're trying to understand their viewpoint. Being seen as impartial earns respect.

They're trustworthy. In real estate, we often learn confidential details of people's lives. People sometimes sell when they're having marital or financial problems, and they don't want anyone to know their private business. They often lean on their agent as a counselor and an understanding shoulder to cry on.

Bobbi   Once clients confide their secrets to me, the information is relegated to the "steel vault" part of my mind; it's a sacred trust. I often wish I didn't know these thorny details. It's not a role I seek, but it's part of the job. I've always found that if I give good, honest advice — sometimes counter to selling their house now — I've earned a client for life.

They foster a cooperative spirit. Team spirit grows when people recognize that success is a collaborative effort. So share the spotlight when others contribute to your project or idea. Be a "big-pie thinker" — someone who puts forward ideas so others can improve them, or simply reinforce that they're good ideas. "Small-pie thinkers" are afraid if they give their ideas away, the pie will run out. We've got news for you: there will always be more pie. Being open to new ideas and collaborating with others gets you so much more than hoarding your little piece.

They take full responsibility for mishaps, even when they weren't directly involved. If you're in charge, the onus is on you. Closing a transaction involves many moving parts: appraisals, inspections, title searches, and more. While not all are handled by the agent, it is the agent's responsibility to oversee each phase of the transaction. Inevitably, something will go wrong. Take ownership of the problem. Don't spend energy laying blame. Put it into finding a solution.

They're calm when others are emotional. How you conduct yourself in stressful situations reveals your true character. Amid the stress of a life-changing event like buying or selling a house, calmness is especially critical. Stress can actually trigger personality changes. Some of the nicest people become absolutely impossible during an escrow. As soon as the transaction closes, they revert to the people you once knew and loved. It helps to remember you're not under personal attack. Your clients are in unfamiliar territory, and their hostility is really masking fear. When people are upset, it helps to let them get it all out before responding.

It's tempting to plunge in, defend your position and explain why it isn't your fault. It's much more professional to remain composed, isolate the problem and work toward a solution. By staying detached from the drama, you can maintain your professional stance, allow others to vent, and then direct their attention to the resolution.

They go the extra mile with a smile. Doing more than the minimum required and giving all the service you can is leading by example. Remember to couple that great service with courtesy. (Don't you just love it when you get great service from a provider who's polite, respectful and appreciative of the chance to serve you?) Add attention to detail, fold in a few effective and efficient systems, sprinkle with a personal touch, and voilà, you've got a winning recipe.

They inspire hope. Of course great leaders face reality, but they're optimistic about the future and they go after it. They share their experience and wisdom with others, and recognize the value of teamwork and togetherness.

2   But first, the basics

Look like you mean it

"A man without a smiling face must not open a shop."

— *Chinese Proverb*

What do people see when they meet you? What's their first impression when you're introduced to them?

The way you present yourself reflects your respect for yourself and the people you meet. People dress differently for different occasions. Of course you wouldn't wear your pajamas to the office, but what is appropriate business wear? Think about your message. You want to convey assurance

Happy Musings
by Sally Huss

Focus on the positive
and the rest will fall away
from lack of interest.

11-30

and inspire confidence, show organization by being put together, and demonstrate your understanding of time-and-place appropriateness. People are attracted to well-groomed people. They actually assume they're more successful, better educated, and better prepared for what they do.

Presentation is also about how you feel when you look good. Dressing professionally makes you feel more confident and shows you're ready to do business. Sloppy clothing, unpolished shoes, and messy hair all say that you don't care much about yourself, and suggest a careless approach to your business and your relationships.

If you want people to have confidence in you, you must show confidence in yourself. A professional appearance helps build trust. When you meet people, look them in the eye and give them your full attention. Offer a firm (not fishy or vise-like) handshake along with a friendly, sincere greeting.

Concentrate on listening more than you speak (it's hard to do!) and give the other person an opportunity to complete thoughts without interrupting. Be curious. Let others know you're interested in what they're saying, and ask questions to show you want to know more. It's important to relate to people on a personal level, but don't get too personal. Always be aware that you're there to conduct business. Be in the moment; leave your own issues behind.

If you use a photo of yourself in your marketing materials, think carefully about what it says about your business. We're always surprised when we flip through real estate magazines and see photos of agents looking provocative, loaded with jewelry, ultra-glamorous or simply unapproachable. Authentic and sincere is the look you want. Consider hiring a portrait photographer, dress professionally, and look straight into the camera with a friendly smile. While posing, think, "I am so glad to meet you!"

Bobbi *You never know where you'll run into a client. Years ago, I popped into the grocery store with my young son one evening. I didn't think about my very casual clothes — jeans, a tee-shirt and a baseball cap. As luck would have it, I ran into a client who didn't immediately recognize me when I introduced her to my son. As I puzzled over this in the car afterward, my son said, "Well, you don't exactly look the way you do during the day!"*

Think about your image before you leave the house, and think about how you'll feel if you run into a client or someone with whom you do, or want to do, business. You don't have to look perfect 24/7, but being clean and put-together is a must when you're in the public eye.

You only get one chance to make a good first impression. If you flunk out the first time, you don't get another shot. Work to make that first good impression, then protect and maintain your image. Your look speaks volumes about you before you say a word. Let your appearance be your professional calling card.

Coddle your cred

Like it or not, your reputation defines you. It's your brand. It sets expectations and validates your skills, experience, and credibility. You earn your reputation on a daily basis. It's not easy to maintain, and it's easily tarnished.

So many areas of life are beyond our control. When things go wrong, everyone's anxious to place blame. Many times it's on us. It's not fair, but then life's not fair. How we handle situations speaks volumes about who we are. Our best advice is to do the right thing every chance you get. That way, even if something goes wrong, people will be more likely to give you

Happy Musings
by Sally Huss
Reliability and credibility
go hand in hand.
Applause will follow.

the benefit of the doubt rather than immediately assuming you're at fault.

Martha We live in a community that requires special open house signs. Out-of of-area agents must have these signs printed to hold their listings open. Over the years, I've developed a reputation for loaning open house signs to these agents. I don't see the point of having them spend money on something they won't soon need again. I do this to be accommodating, with no strings attached. Interestingly enough, I've taken several nice listings over the years when those same agents got tired of driving and wasting valuable time in an area that wasn't their focus. Do the right thing, and good things will come to you.

A good reputation defines who you are, creates demand, and becomes a bankable asset. As a real estate agent, your reputation consists primarily of your skills, experience, and word-of of-mouth referrals. Every time you make a move, you validate the opinions your family, friends, and peers have about you. Having a good reputation means that you've maintained a high degree of credibility, you're a positive influence on others, and you hold yourself to higher standards.

Be aware of your reputation at all times. Show respect to everyone you come in contact with. Smile and be courteous. You'll feel better, look better, and find life is much more fun.

When you hold an open house, assume every visitor is a friend of the owners. That way, you'll always put your best foot forward and keep the seller's best interest at heart. If a home you're showing truly doesn't work for the prospects, follow up to help them find the right home. New home builders hire "shoppers" to visit their sale offices and check up on the salespeople. They report back on the agent's sales skills, tract knowledge, and overall performance. If you tell yourself every visitor is "shopping" you on behalf of the owner, your presentation will always be far more polished and professional.

Being respectful includes listening actively to what people are saying to you. It's easy to put your own agenda out front, but success lies in understanding and respecting the positions of others. Being on time shows tremendous respect. Everyone has a full schedule. If you think what you do is more important than what anyone else does, you're wrong.

Respectful people interact with others in a constructive way. They don't indulge in gossip by spreading or even listening to rumors. Some people thrive on gossip and revel in the misfortunes of others. If you aren't open to hearing it, the gossipers won't feel comfortable bringing it to you.

Work as if you own your own company, because you do. Treat everyone like a customer, including your co-workers. Are you easy to do business with? Are you approachable?

Take responsibility for your actions or lack of them. You will make mistakes. It's vital to own up to them and face the music. It's best to make these apologies in person. It's difficult for people to stay angry or upset when you look them in the eye and say "I'm sorry. I let you down." This is a critical part of building a good reputation. Things go wrong for all of us. It's how we handle the situation that sets us apart from the crowd.

Choose your battles. Always take the high road. That's sometimes easier said than done, but it always works out for the best. Not every wrong can be made right. Not every fight is worth fighting. Fight the ones that mean something, and walk away from the rest. It's so much easier on you if you can walk away without expending negative energy.

By no means are we suggesting you run from problems. We can be quite the she-bears when it comes to defending the people and things we hold dear, and we're vigorous champions of all that is right and worth defending. We simply recognize that not all issues have an impact on us or ours, and not all victories will make a difference that matters. We don't fight just because we feel we're right and need to win. We fight to protect what needs to be protected, and when it matters. Otherwise, we try to focus on more positive, proactive uses of our time.

If this chapter sounds preachy, please forgive us. As we write this, we're remembering a number of times we could have handled situations better, made better decisions, or simply been better people ... and thinking of ways to prevent the same things from happening in the future. We, too, will grow from writing and reading this.

No offense: you should be committed

"It is our choices…that show what we truly are, far more than our abilities."

– J.K. Rowling

We all make countless decisions each day. Being able to make quick yet well- thought-out decisions is critical to getting things done. We base our decisions on available information combined with our experiences and gut feelings. If we procrastinate, we risk looking insecure and unable to make a commitment. If we avoid making a decision altogether, someone else may make it for us — and it may not be the one we wanted.

If you've made a decision and new information forces you to reconsider, change your mind only if absolutely necessary. Politicians who flip-flop on issues based on the current polls not only create confusion about where they stand, but show a lack of core values. When you constantly change your mind, it looks like you either don't know what you're doing or you're trying to please everyone instead of doing what needs to be done, regardless of the fallout.

Opinions are everywhere. If you're easily influenced by others, you won't listen to your own good sense. Seek advice from people you trust. Not only those who have more knowledge and experience on the subject, but those who have your best interests — not their own agendas — in mind.

It takes courage to reach a decision. Doing it quickly and definitively shows that you understand the impact of your choice and you're prepared to accept the consequences. When your words and actions consistently reflect your core principals, it shows you know what you're doing and why.

Don't give in to giving up

"I know the price of success: dedication, hard work, and an unremitting devotion to the things you want to see happen."
— *Frank Lloyd Wright*

Like decision making, persistence is a commitment — the determination to complete what you begin. It can be cultivated with a combination of willpower and desire. Try baby steps to get you going. Use daily lists to keep you on track. Surround yourself with people you trust who will encourage you to keep going until you reach your goal. Ask them to hold you accountable for hanging in there. If you can get past a little failure and rejection, you'll reap the rewards you deserve. Know that defeat is only temporary. History is filled with accounts of people who failed countless times before breaking through. You can do it!

Know the drill

Whatever your business, you're expected to perform, and pressure mounts as you get closer to the deadline. You might have a project due, a proposal to make, a speech to deliver, or a listing presentation coming up. You know it's out there and you know it's important, but you plan to get to it later, when you have more time.

Confidence is all about being prepared. When faced with an appointment or assignment, it's usually best to attack it right away, while it's fresh in your mind and you have a pocket of time to get at least a chunk of it done. If you put it aside, your time will likely be consumed with countless other things. Then you'll be under pressure, the quality of your work may slip — or worse, you'll be forced to fake it.

Have all the information you need at hand and the paperwork done in advance. Prepare up, down and sideways so you'll feel comfortable discussing any question you get. You may not have the advantage of knowing the client or audience until you get there, so have several approaches at the ready.

People process information in different ways. You want to be able to tailor your approach to a variety of learning styles. Even if you don't need all this preparation, it's comforting to know it's at your fingertips, just in case.

Some agents walk into a listing interview with a notepad and a business card. That's it, nothing else. We don't know what kind of preparation went into that appointment, but clearly they didn't give themselves the best advantage. Being well-prepared and having everything you need to get the job done at that moment shows professionalism and inspires confidence. It feels good to know you've got it down.

Bobbi *It helps me to do a little role reversal before I go on an appointment. I put myself in my buyer's or seller's shoes and think about what questions they might ask me. I don't want to be blindsided and dumbstruck if they ask, "What makes you different from the other agents working in this area?" I want to think about my point of differentiation in advance, so I can answer easily and with confidence. Once in a while, I get a question I've never been asked before. "Wow, that's a great question! I'm going to write that one down. Let me find out and get right back to you!"*

Have you ever winged it? Scary, huh? The Boy Scouts got it right: Be Prepared.

Communication, or static?

Swallow the frog. What does this silly phrase mean? It usually means having to make a tough phone call. Something has happened that needs to be discussed. It might not be pleasant. It might not be what the other person wants to hear. But putting it off will only make the situation worse. A real estate example might be, "The buyer needs to close a week later." This touches off a cascade of events: rescheduling moving vans, furniture deliveries, utility transfers, etc. But the more you delay delivery of this news, the bigger the problems become.

We talk about the importance of good communication skills all the time. In fact, today's information superhighway makes it nearly impossible to avoid communicating. And yet, poor communication is still a common customer service complaint. Why don't we do a better job of it?

Communication is made up of two parts: the message and how the message is delivered. The second part is the hard one. It takes skill and a measure of finesse to ensure that your message is heard clearly and received as intended.

The illusion of communication can fool you. You think you're truly getting it, yet each of you walks away with a different understanding. How can that be? Next time you're in a conversation, listen carefully and ask what the other person means by certain key phrases. It might surprise you to learn their words meant something different than you thought they did. Force yourself to slow down, listen, and not make assumptions. Give the communicator a chance to explain the message so you truly understand what's being said.

One technique is to ask a question rather than assume you already know the answer. This can take courage; you might worry you'll sound dumb for asking. Sometimes it's as simple as saying, "I'm sorry, I'm not sure I understand what you meant by _____. Or, "Could you tell me a little more about that?"

Listening more than speaking takes discipline. But if you patiently allow the other party to finish a thought completely, you'll reach a better understanding. It's almost irresistible to interrupt, complete someone's sentences, or jump into the conversation the moment the other person takes a breath. But when you interrupt, you're implying, "Yeah, yeah, I already know where this is going." Instead of forming your response in your head before the other party has finished speaking, really listen. Allow the person to complete the thought, then pause. This shows you're thoughtfully considering what's been said before you respond. Not only will you get to know people better, you'll gain their respect.

In cases where you're expected to communicate on a regular basis, you might only need to let your client, friend or relative know there's nothing new going on. "I'm thinking about you, and wish I had something exciting to report. When you have a chance, please call and let me know what's going on with you." Or, "You may have noticed that I haven't sold your house yet — not for lack of trying! Please call me if you have questions or concerns." Simply reach out to them so they don't feel ignored.

Never, ever dismiss the importance of the hand-written note. Phone calls and emails have their place, but old-school putting pen to paper still has a time-honored role. We mail holiday and birthday cards for a reason. They're personal and require thought and time. Nothing is more valuable than giving another person your time, because we all have a limited amount of it. When you let people know they have your undivided attention, it's remembered, appreciated, and just plain good business.

Beware of procrastination swamp

"The search for the perfect venture can turn into procrastination. Your idea may or may not have merit. The key is to get started."

–Unknown Author

Martha: I've been trying to address this topic all week, but I just couldn't seem to get going. There's always so much else that needs to be done.

OK, I'm back for another stab at it. Somehow, the title has become self-fulfilling. But I can't give up. It's got to be done, and now it's become a burden.

Sound familiar? Of course it does. We all procrastinate at one time or another. The solution to this problem is different for everyone. When I'm faced with a daunting project that I can't seem to get off the ground, I break it down into manageable sections. Nibbling away on small bites helps get me started. (You need a game plan and a deadline to really make this approach work.)

When I first started providing Broker Price Opinions for relocation moves, each one was a huge task that could spread out over an entire day, or in some cases several days. Every phone call was a welcome reprieve. In fact, I looked for excuses to do anything but the job at hand. Eventually, I faced the fact that I was wasting precious time pretending to get the job done.

The process is so simple now. First, I determine the three closest competitive properties currently on the market or in escrow. Then I pick the three best recent comparable (closed) sales. That's it for Day One. It takes minutes, and that portion of the program is complete.

The next morning, I get up a little earlier than usual and sit at the computer with my cup of coffee and fill in the blanks. At this time of day, I can count on zero phone calls, emails, and distractions in general. I'm fresh and focused, and I can complete the job in half an hour. This is also a great way to propel myself into my day. I check something off my list early, and it totally energizes and empowers me to win the entire day.

Early morning might not work for you. It may be your least focused, least effective time of day. But if you put your mind to it, you'll identify a plan that will work for you. When you find your own "sweet spot" for getting things done, plan your day around it.

Well, what do you expect?

"Climate is what we expect, weather is what we get."

— Mark Twain

Has this ever happened to you? You're sure you did a good job, and yet your client was less than pleased with the results. We learned the hard way that if we don't set mutually agreed-on expectations, things can go sideways in a hurry. Here's an example of how un-set expectations equal un-met expectations.

Bobbi *I listed a house for sale and coordinated a showing time with my sellers, arranging to meet the buyers and their agent at the house. So far, so good. But I didn't nail down the rest of the ground rules, the client's expectations weren't met, and I almost lost a good relationship.*

As I was driving to the house to meet the buyers, their agent called to say she had to cancel the appointment. I grabbed my cell phone and left messages about the cancellation on all of my seller's contact numbers, and left. What a big mistake! The sellers had done a fabulous job of preparing for the showing, lighting candles and the fireplaces and turning on all the lights. Since I never went into the house, the lights remained on and the candles and fireplaces kept on burning. (I'm lucky there wasn't a fire.)

When my sellers came home, they were understandably upset. They'd assumed I'd go inside to de-stage the home after the appointment cancellation. But we simply hadn't discussed their plans to stage the home so completely for showings. We didn't talk about what should happen if an appointment were canceled. Needless to say, I felt like an idiot, and learned a tough lesson that day. It won't ever happen again.

Sometimes we don't establish detailed expectations with our clients because it's easier not to. But when we haven't been crystal clear, there's a big risk of confusion and disappointment. Expectations must be acknowledged and understood by everyone involved. They become a benchmark and help to clarify your relationship.

For example, a seller might want public open houses to be held during the listing term. That may sound pretty clear, but a few more questions are in order to make sure everyone is on the same wavelength. How many open houses, what days, during what hours? Keep probing until everyone understands what will be happening and when. You'll both have the same expectation, and be happy with the results.

For example, it's important to recommend a regular review of the market with your sellers during the listing term until the home is sold. You may view this meeting as a time to compare competing houses for sale and recently sold homes — data that often points to the need for a competitive price reduction. But if you don't make this expectation clear in advance, your sellers may not see it that way. They may want to talk about additional advertising, not adjusting the price to the market.

Set the expectation for the meeting in advance: "We'll look at what's new on the market and what's gone into escrow each week. If we aren't getting showings or offers, we may need to adjust the price." It's far less stressful to be ahead of the curve and anticipate the trouble spots rather than get stuck in a defensive position. If you marry your communication with your service, you'll deliver the results you promised.

Think, think, think

"Avoid the crowd. Do your own thinking independently. Be the chess player, not the chess piece."

- Ralph Charell

If you want to get more done in less time, stop and think before you start. Ask yourself: Is there a better way to do this? Can I be more efficient? Cost effective? Faster? Do I really even need to do this? You'd be amazed how a little thought and a few changes can streamline almost anything.

Martha   Before I leave the house, I think about where I'm going that day and what I'll pass on the way. It's frustrating to drive by the only place in town where I can get replacement batteries/ink cartridges/prescriptions and not have the information I need to do it. On a well-planned day, you can fit in a myriad of little errands without feeling the grind.

My friends love to tease me about my driving. I'm always lost in thought; even if they wave frantically, I rarely notice them. The truth is, I'm busy thinking. I'm thinking about my next appointment and how it's going to play out. I'm searching for that little point of differentiation that will set me apart from my competition. I'm pondering names and details and making lists in my head. I usually don't listen to music or anything distracting while I drive. I want to concentrate on my own thoughts, which are distracting enough. (Some part of me must pay attention to the road!)

Walking is another great opportunity to think. In a single 30-45 minute walk, I can pose questions and answer them, plan parties, design menus, and solve the problems of my world. In fact, this book was born on a walk. I gave a lot of thought to writing it, and got the idea of collaborating with Bobbi while striding along.

3 Address your stress

Staying sane

"The statistics on sanity are that one out of every four Americans is suffering from some form of mental illness. Think of your three best friends. If they're okay, then it's you."

— Rita Mae Brown

Martha *Years ago I knew the contents of every drawer in my home and every item in my cupboards and pantry, including the expiration dates. But I was a stay-at at-home mom with one baby in a two-bedroom condo. I could really get my arms around my life. As time marched on, I complicated things with more kids, a more-than-full-time*

Happy Musings
by Sally Huss
You can't go wrong,
if you keep goin',
as long as you're goin'
with life.

job, a bigger house, multiple family commitments, and numerous family activities. Giving up that control — and the need to be perfect — was essential to survival.

Getting to no

You want to please. You want to be an overachiever. But eventually, you can't keep up the pace, and you let yourself and others down. Then you feel guilty, and everyone suffers. You say yes to people because you're wired that way, but you have a right to say no.

Stop and think before you respond with an immediate yes. Maybe there's an alternative. Bring cookies to school for the Halloween party? Ask if you may make a donation to the party instead. People are already spending time planning and executing it. They're already in party mode at the store. It's easy for them to pick something up on your behalf. Now you've donated and been a part of the party without adding another thing to your list of to-do's and your hectic schedule — and without saying no.

Create a policy or guideline that makes saying no easier. When asked to contribute to a cause or an organization, stop and think. Does it fit into your plan? If it doesn't, don't let guilt color your decision. If you're asked to advertise in a school bulletin or sports schedule, practice saying, " I'm sorry, I've already allocated my charitable contributions/advertising budget for this year." You'll sound so organized and corporate saying no that the person soliciting you will feel good about it!

Written goals and strategies also make it easier to make a decision. "Thanks, but I'm putting my energy and budget into attracting Internet leads. I won't be advertising in your publication at this time." If the contact persists, repeat your position in a slightly different way. Keep your answers short and to the point. You don't have to justify your position to anyone. Be polite, but firm. Giving false hope ("Yes, you can try me again next month") won't do either of you any favors.

When asked to join a group or sit on a committee, take a deep breath and say, "Let me check my calendar. I don't want to commit to something I can't give my full attention to." If it turns out it does work for you, it's easy to respond with a yes. When in doubt, say no. If you change your mind, it's very easy to go from "no" to "yes," but very difficult and disappointing to do the reverse.

One final thought: It's time to quit organizations that aren't contributing to your advancement, your network, or your enjoyment. Take stock of your commitments and just say no when you need to.

Losing it? Start moving it

"The sovereign invigorator of the body is exercise, and of all the exercises walking is the best."

– Thomas Jefferson

A must, no exceptions: You simply have to find a way to move around in some fashion three or four times a week for a minimum of at least half an hour. Let's face it: our days demand an exorbitant amount of energy. Even a small helping of exercise will make a huge difference in your energy level.

We both love to walk. When you walk by yourself, you have time to think through projects, strategize goals, and formulate plans. Walking with a friend becomes a wonderful therapy session.

Walking is good for your heart and your muscles, wards off osteoporosis, and fills your soul. It's free, and can be done anywhere. Bad weather? Hit the mall and walk. Can't leave the house? March in front of the TV while you watch a half-hour program. You don't even need a treadmill.

You don't need weights to add a little weight training, either. Check out the pantry and hoist whatever you see that's the appropriate weight. Anytime, any place, any kind of movement works. No excuses. It's crucial.

Martha: Find a form of exercise that works for you and stick to it. For some it's a home gym. I have had very serious machines in my home over the years, but I wasn't able to maintain a regular routine. I have signed up with gyms, but I find them intimidating.

I joined Curves five years ago and I have stayed on a reasonably routine schedule of three times a week. One half hour at a time, chatting with friends, hearing fun music, shoring up my energy level, and generally feeling good about myself. Many times I've left work just dragging and a quick stop at Curves has left me feeling invigorated again. No matter how crazy my days are, I've committed to such a simple exercise program that I absolutely cannot fail.

Find yours.

4 Simple tricks

Rituals and systems

"Management works in the system; leadership works on the system."

–Kahlil Gibran

It goes without saying that children's bedtimes go more smoothly with rituals in place: Brush teeth, potty, bedtime story, kisses. What needs to be said is this strategy works for all ages. Everything is smoother with rituals and systems in place.

Happy Musings
by Sally Huss
Our gift is time.
Our gift in return
is to use it wisely.

©2007 Sally Huss, Dist. by King Features Syndicate

Martha *My mornings are filled with them. One of the first is to start the coffee. When I moved on after fifteen years of marriage, I found myself alone in a new kitchen, faced with making coffee for one. It was just too sad to continue the comfortable ritual I'd been used to for years.*

I decided I needed to reprogram my morning. I got rid of my Mr. Coffee and went out and bought a French coffee press. Scented candles were now involved. My new ritual was still very simple, but suddenly it was very much on purpose. This easy change gave me a fresh outlook on my day. I'm happy to report that I've recovered sufficiently to start my day with an automatic coffee maker again. Scented candles continue to be involved.

If rituals are soothing, systems are critical. Every recurring detail of your multifaceted life should fall into a system.

Martha *When I was raising my family, I had a simple one for laundry. Every morning I threw a load in the washer, alternating light and dark each day. After work, I moved the load to the dryer. I'm ashamed to admit we dressed out of the dryer many mornings, eliminating the need for much folding or putting away. OK, it wasn't a perfect system, but it got the job done, and the laundry never piled up.*

I have a system for putting on makeup. It takes about two minutes. The foundation and blush follow the moisturizer/ sun block; the eyebrows, mascara, and shadow come next. If I somehow get side sidetracked and out of order, I veer hopelessly off track with no prospect of recovery. I risk heading out into the world sans a critical component. (Gasp!) I don't have a structure for going back and filling in the gaps. Maybe my system could use a little overhaul.

My online banking system has been in place since the mid-1990s. It was a fairly new idea when I started, and everyone warned me of the dangers lurking on the Internet. I've never had any problems. All my creditors have accounts, and everything with a consistent regular payment is paid automatically. Bills with fluctuating balances, like utilities, take only a few moments to pay. I encourage my tenants to use auto pay instead of mailing their rent; it saves me extra trips to the bank. This plan not only saves time, it eliminates the pain usually associated with paying bills. They get paid in spite of me.

Structure is critical to keeping your business running smoothly and your blood pressure in check. We know agents who had three listings and decided to turn down a fourth because it was just too much work! Three listings will require the same effort as thirty if you systematize everything, from New Listing Checklist to Client Follow-up.

Use lists for every system. When you meet prospects, their data goes into your prospect system. When they convert to a listing or a sale, you move to a checklist for listing procedures or escrow timelines. Commit these lists to paper so you always have a track record of your accomplishments and a paper trail of your progress. Now repeat the procedure again … and again … until you build momentum and your system becomes a habit.

Without systems in place, you have to reinvent the process each time. With them, you can accomplish so many tasks on autopilot. Streamline and simplify on a regular basis. Rememer to ask yourself, "Can this be simpler, quicker, more cost cost-effective?"

Write it down, check it off

Always, always keep a spiral notebook handy. Isn't it frustrating to have a great idea flash through your mind — in one side and out the other? If you don't write it down the moment it occurs to you, you may not be able to retrieve that life-changing thought later.

Don't think that keeping a notebook means you're flighty and forgetful. Do it because so much happens in a day, you'd lose track of all the loose ends without it. The contents can range from important goal-oriented thoughts to "remember to pick up at Target" notes. Brainstorm in quiet moments and write down proactive ideas and major to-do lists just to push yourself. Keep your notebook by your bed, because great ideas can come to you in the night when your mind isn't so busy.

This matter-of-fact discipline will become a part of you. It's amazingly easy to get into the habit of writing everything down in the same place. No more loose scraps of paper,

Post-It® notes or backs of envelopes to chase down. It's also an easy habit to sustain, because it's simple and it works.

You might want to use a BlackBerry or PDA to track your contact list, calendar, and so forth. But you may find that not everything needs to be there. Some phone numbers will live in both the BlackBerry/PDA and the notebook. Names and numbers of clients, associates, and affiliates you're working with during an escrow go on the list. Not all of them have to be in the BlackBerry forever. But you need the numbers you are currently using in plain sight where they're easily retrievable. "Out of sight, out of mind" is a classic saying for a reason.

In addition to a trusty notebook, try using a simple checklist of daily to-do's. It's the same list every day, and it includes very simple and seemingly mindless activities like taking your vitamins. It will help you to stay on track in all areas of your life.

Daily Checklist

__ Do my 10/10 (10 gratitude/10 positive actions)

__ Take vitamins

__ Exercise

__ Check the news

__ Review my goals

__ Review Vision Board

__ Review appointments for the day

__ Make a difficult phone call

__ Review MLS hotsheet

__ Update clients

__ Follow-up on a lead

__ Check email

__ Send a proactive email

__ Compliment someone

__ Make someone's day

__ Send a note card

__ Make a healthy food choice

__ Contact a family member

__ Read a few pages of a self-development book

__ Return every phone call

__ Do something for myself

__ Drink water

__ Plan a social event

__ Set up tomorrow's day

A printable copy of this checklist is available on our website at
www.RealLessonsAndLaughs.com

Here's why some of the those tasks made the list.

If you're like we are, you don't automatically drink water. You go all day until you're suffering with a dehydration headache. You don't recognize it for what it is, so you have a cup of coffee as a little jump start and become further dehydrated. Or you think you're hungry instead of thirsty, so you eat. By listing it as a task, you're reminded each time you review the list to drink water. You can check it off no matter how much you drink, just because you did it and it encourages you to continue the habit.

List contacting your family so you'll always be reaching out to the people you love.

List your hobbies and interests to keep them in front of you. Likewise a myriad of projects you want to keep advancing down the field.

One of the most productive entries is making a difficult phone call. We all have those dreaded calls that we put off as long as possible, allowing them to sap our energy while we prolong the agony. Make just one so you can check it off. You'll feel so energized, you'll make a few more while you're still feeling psyched.

You don't have to check off every item every day. Use your list to help maintain balance in all areas of your life: business, personal, health, hobbies. Progress will be made a little at a time, and in this simple way, you'll keep your not-so-simple life goals in the spotlight.

By the way, once you're habitually carrying your notebook and your list, make sure you always have a pen that works. Have you noticed that in every household, the pen next to the phone rarely works? When your pen dies, toss it out or replace the cartridge. It won't heal itself back in the drawer.

Let somebody else do it

"When in charge ponder. When in trouble delegate. When in doubt mumble."

– Author Unknown

Even for those who have learned to delegate over the years, it's still not easy. There are so many excuses, all flimsy.

- I can do it better than someone else.

- I don't have time to train someone right now. I'll wait until I'm not so busy.

- I can't add to anyone else's responsibility.

- There's no one available to delegate to.

- I like doing this task.

- I'd have the job done by the time I explained it.

Good employees and assistants want to take on more responsibilities. It makes them more valuable and their jobs more interesting. Valuable staff members want to learn more about the job. It does take time to stop and train someone, but it pays huge dividends in time-saving and productivity over the long term. You may even find someone else can do the job better than you do.

Before you delegate, determine whether the job is even necessary. Don't delegate busy work that could be eliminated. Do delegate recurring and routine activities. Fact-finding and collecting data, preparation of paperwork, copying, collating, mail, and data entry are all perfect activities to delegate to others.

Martha When I hire people, I ask them to list their strengths and describe what they consider to be a perfect workday. Everyone has a favorite part of the day and a task they look forward to. If you assign activities that play to their strengths, you have happy, productive employees who do a better job than you or anyone else would. Fill in the gaps by assigning alternate responsibilities to someone else, or by outsourcing them.

Don't micromanage. There are usually several different ways to accomplish the desired result. You might just learn something if you get out of the way.

Give praise and feedback where it's appropriate, and offer further training as needed. Be sure you've explained the requirements thoroughly. Some people know how to do the job, but not how to explain it to someone else. You're setting yourself and your employee up for failure if you don't take time to explain the process. Ultimately, the finished product is your responsibility — so managing the delegation process is critical to both its success and yours.

Then just let go.

Get rid of the time robbers

"I recommend you take care of the minutes; for hours will take care of themselves."

— *Philip Dormer Stanhope*

They say everyone has the same 24 hours in a day, but some of us suspect that we were given more. You need never run out of time. It's a wonderful gift, since life is so full of interesting things to do. You'd never want to miss out on something for lack of time. So your admission from today forward isn't, "I ran out of time." It's, "I didn't make time." It's simply a choice!

Having plenty of time is easy. You just need to be aware of time throughout the day — and be merciless to the time robbers.

Phone calls and emails

Watch your minutes carefully, since they quickly become hours. The telephone and email inbox can consume your day if you let them. Yet with a little effort and a bit of forethought, they can make your day.

On business days, try to limit most phone calls to a minute. If you have sixty one-minute calls a day, you will have spoken on the phone for one full hour by the last call. If those same calls take three minutes each, you've spent three full hours of your day on the phone. It's amazing when you think about it!

Obviously, it isn't possible to keep each call within that time frame. Learning to subtly make the other person aware of the start and finish of a conversation can make a difference. Using vocal nuances or well-chosen words will (hopefully) let the person on the other end know you're wrapping it up. It's very effective to repeat the high point of the conversation, define what's expected after you hang up, and say your goodbyes.

"Thanks for the information. I'll call escrow, make the change, and have paperwork sent to you. Let me know when you have signatures ready." Thanks and goodbye. There's no need to restate, rehash, or rethink the information. Be succinct and clear about what's expected, and hang up.

This has the same effect as standing up when you're talking in person. The conversation is winding up, and we must say our goodbyes now. This is not selfish. Those you are speaking with have only so many minutes in their days as well. Out of respect for their time, speak quickly and get to the point right away.

Voicemail

Please use voicemail for its intended purpose. Leave clear, succinct messages with your question and/or information and your phone number. We recommend leaving your phone number at both the beginning of your message and the end. Try to encourage others to extend the same courtesy and efficiency when leaving messages for you.

"Hello, this is _____ with XYZ Company at (phone number). I'm calling regarding your listing at _____ Avenue. I have clients interested in that home, but they'll need some seller-assisted financing. Are the sellers in a position — and would they be willing — to carry back a 10% second on the property? Please call me if you think that might be a possibility. My number is _____."

In a perfect world, the return call would go something like this:

"This is _____ , at (phone number), and I'm returning your call regarding _____. I've spoken to the sellers and confirmed that they do have enough equity to carry a second. Based on the entire offer and pending a review of the financial strength of the buyers, they'd consider that option. Please let me know if you have any further questions. It would be my pleasure to enter an escrow with you. Once again my number is _____"

Bobbi *When I get calls from people saying they have questions for me, I inevitably get their voicemails when I return the calls. If I'd known what the question was, I could have left an answer and we could both have moved forward. Get in the habit of leaving a complete, detailed message or a call to action, and move on. When I get a message saying "tag, you're it," I don't play the game. There's not enough time in the day to waste on that.*

Martha *I handle calls and emails ten at a time. That doesn't mean I wait until I have ten messages. It means that I return the calls and emails that are waiting, make a few calls and emails to generate business or proactively move my life forward, then call or email a friend or family* *member just to check in quickly and make a connection. It only takes a few minutes more, and it accomplishes so much in terms of effective communication and maintaining relationships.*

Those endless errands

Run your errands in a circle. Whenever you get into the car, take stock of your to do's. What stops can you make on the way? What can be checked off your list quickly and painlessly? Life rarely runs in a straight line when you think ahead.

An example might be running out at lunch to pick up a sandwich. You could leave the office, take a straight shot to the deli, and return to work the same way. Or you could drive in a circle and make several stops. If you pass a friend's or former client's home, stop in for a quick hello. They'll appreciate your thinking of them, and it gives you a chance to network and ask for referrals. In not many more minutes, you've managed to pick up lunch, check several to do's off of your list, and re-connect with a contact or two for possible leads.

It would be even more efficient if you called in your order before you left the office. In that case, you could conceivably take care of a few errands, do a little prospecting, and have lunch in the same amount of time. Now we're talking big win in the race against time! There's only so much of it, so take full advantage of every single minute.

Martha I have a staging area in my home and one at my office. At home, it's the desk I pass as I walk to my car, and the car itself. Anything that needs to leave the house goes to the staging area: a book or dish to return to a friend, clothes for the cleaners, store returns, jewelry or shoes in need of repair. Eventually I'll be driving past the destination, and it's so much less frustrating to have the item with me and check it off the list.

At the office, it's the right front corner of my desk. As I prepare mail or complete a project, I move the material to that spot. When I leave my office, I pick up the pile and drop the items off at the appropriate destinations. Mail gets mailed throughout the day, and I clear my desk and move projects forward smoothly. It's not only an efficient habit to get into, but it gives you such a sense of accomplishment to see paper (your job!) moving forward.

A dearth of deadlines

Sounds like a good thing, right? Wrong. Have you ever noticed how much more you get done on the day before you leave on vacation? That's the power of a deadline. It makes sense that we can attain that same level of efficiency anytime just by setting up a time limit. Try thinking in fifteen-minute increments. It's not only very helpful when you're keeping track of your minutes, it also adds a little sense of urgency by giving you a deadline for every task.

Kids and careers

"You can be a wonderful woman, but you can't be Wonder Woman. She was a fictional character."

— *Unknown*

If you're raising a family, you're probably struggling harder to find balance now than you will at any other time in your life. There's just not enough time to handle everything and help everyone who needs your attention. If you're working outside the home, it's nearly impossible to stay ahead of the curve. Nearly, but not totally. You have to pay attention to the minutes and be constantly thinking, but you can handle it. It won't be easy and it won't be perfect, but you can bring balance to your life.

This is easier to say if your children are grown. Juggling young children's schedules along with your own is extremely difficult. Clients just don't want to hear that your son's ballgame is starting. They want your full attention, and yes, they deserve it.

Martha   *During my seemingly endless years of raising kids, it was a constant battle to stay on top of the vitally important issues. Just when I got used to the phase one child was going through, a new phase for the other one developed. I decided my only choice was to take it day by day and not sweat the small stuff. I know it's a cliché, but there's a reason we have these sayings.*

Looking back, I can honestly tell you it doesn't matter how your children dress (provided it's appropriate for current weather conditions and dress codes). What I mean is, the outfit really doesn't have to match. The hair doesn't require a matching bow. If the children are happy, you would do yourself a favor to get happy, too.

Lay out entire outfits the night before, including both shoes. If anyone is involved in an after school activity requiring uniforms or gear, make sure it's all in the staging area. Go through homework and teacher handouts. Load everything back into the backpack and leave it in the staging area before bedtime.

Speaking of bedtime, there should be one. Routine is critical to balance, and bedtime is the most important routine of the day. As you work your way through the process – pajamas on, brush teeth, read a book, kiss goodnight — kids wind down and get ready to fall asleep. They understand the day is over. It seems so civilized. But admittedly, it's easier said than done.

Lunches can be made, individually wrapped, and frozen for the week ahead. So can cookies. Boxed drinks can be frozen, too. In the morning, all you have to do is grab a bag, toss in one of each plus a piece of fruit, and you're done. Keep a running grocery list. As you use up an item, put it on the list. In fact, do this for all your shopping.

Mornings are critical to the day's balance. You absolutely must be up well before anyone else. This could be your blissful few minutes of alone time, the one and only thing that keeps you sane. You need and deserve time to yourself. Throw in a load of laundry, make coffee, read the paper, take a walk. At the end of your personal time, load the wet clothes into the dryer, put the lunches together and put them in the staging area. Take a shower and get dressed before the children have to start getting ready. You'll be relaxed and helpful instead of stressed and frantic.

Finally, leave some white space in your daily schedule. Drive time, interruptions, and previously unforeseen issues pop up all day long. Having some flex time built in makes it possible to maintain your cool. That, plus making a lot of sincere apologies to your children and their coaches for always being the last parent to pick them up from practice.

Oh yes, and remember to breathe. That helps, too.

Toughness: bad for beef, good for business

"It is how you deal with failure that determines how you achieve success."

—David Feherty

To succeed in sales, as in life, you need mental toughness and resiliency. You've heard all the stories about famous and successful people who failed — Lincoln and his many defeats, Churchill and the numerous setbacks he faced in his career. (He truly lived his famous quote, "Never, never, never give up.")

Happy Musings
by Sally Huss

Hard bodies are better
with soft hearts.

© 2006 Sally Huss, Dist. by King Features Syndicate   11-2

One of the best-known success-through-failure stories is Edison's. His inventions failed countless times, yet he went down in history as one of the most successful and life-changing inventors in history.

In sales, you have to learn to take the good with the bad. Rejection is a fact of life. Top producers have more going for them, so when they don't get the listing or their offer isn't accepted, they have more business to fall back on. New or struggling agents can see their entire business model crumble with a single "no."

The obvious answer is to get ramped up to the point where "no" isn't devastating. It can still hurt; you aren't expected to be completely thick-skinned. Don't believe setbacks should be taken lightly. Do believe they can be huge learning experiences.

Every now and then, you're rejected when you thought you had a tremendous connection with the client. You were already spending the commission! Big mistake. Our competition is excellent, and there's always the chance someone else will connect better than you do. Maybe it's just timing. Or you remind them of someone they don't like. Try to come to terms with the fact that you can never win them all.

Occasionally, you'll be passed over several times in a row. When that happens, you have to acknowledge you're not performing to your full capacity. Call the client and say, "I understand you've chosen to go in another direction. To improve my skills, I'd love to hear what I could have done to earn your business." Many times there's a valid reason — the chosen agent was referred by a respected friend or colleague, or the two have a history together.

Other times, there isn't. That's when you know in your heart that you could have done a better job, and you step back and honestly assess your presentation. You may have been lazy and not researched thoroughly enough. You may not have shown enough enthusiasm for the home and/or the opportunity. We all wear out from time to time, and we pay dearly for it.

Self-talk is critical to successfully overcoming rejection. If you know you gave it your best shot, tell yourself so with absolute confidence. Take full responsibility for the setback, and make a conscious decision to prevail. Accept that adversity comes with the program, and recommit to keeping at it until victory is yours. After a rejection, plan your next two victories. Review your goals and your business plan, and decide what you'll do to generate two contracts for the one you lost.

The fear of rejection will cripple you if you give in to it. Realize the fear of making the call or contact is worse than the act itself. Like anything else, it gets easier with practice. Desensitize yourself by doing it over and over. Push through the fear until you reach success. It's so much easier than living with the fearful, anxious feeling caused by not doing what must be done.

Is anybody out there?

"At times our own candle goes out and is rekindled by a spark from another person. Each of us has cause to think with deep gratitude of those who have lighted the flame within us."

–Albert Schweitzer

One very real price outside salespeople pay is loneliness. True, we do form strong bonds with our clients while we're working together. We see each other often and communicate frequently. We get to know each other and become close. But we're in people's lives to conduct business, not to be their buddies. We're professional counselors, and the trust we earn is sacred. Sellers move out of the area. Buyers turn their attention to their day-to-day lives. The ebb and flow of clients is a natural thing.

Unlike office workers who interact with their colleagues eight hours a day, five days a week, we do most of our business away from the office. We meet with sellers in their homes, often on the weekend or in the evening when they're available. During the day, we're previewing and showing homes, meeting with lenders, title reps, escrow officers, inspectors, appraisers — all away from our office bases. Successful salespeople don't hang out in their offices just to chat by the proverbial water cooler. Time is too precious. When they're in the office, they're working — on the phone, conducting meetings in the conference room, preparing for appointments.

How do you cope with the feeling of isolation you get when you're on your own so much? For us, it's about staying connected with friends and family and making time for ourselves. Schedule appointments for personal time just as you do for work. If you don't, you'll get cranky and feel used up. You need connection time to feel balanced and healthy.

It can be addicting to work long hours, and it begins to creep into defining who you are. You want to accomplish more, more, more, and forget to take time to appreciate each day. But if the soul isn't fed, your supply of energy diminishes, along with your ability to accomplish everything you have to do.

To avoid this trap, try to schedule things you want to do along with things you need to do. That way, finding time for taking care of yourself and connecting with people you care about isn't left to chance. You'll be much happier and more productive if you sprinkle a little bit of fun in along with your work.

Bobbi *To me, loneliness is a place. It is a place that I can allow myself to fall into and a place I can take myself out of. That brings me to my squirrels. This may sound silly but I love my squirrels. I have a family of them that live behind a hedge in my backyard. I can see them from my home office. I feed them and (I hate to admit this) I have names for them—Grey Shawl, Savannah, and Shy Guy. I know they were fine fending for themselves before I got here but I like to think they enjoy being my "pets." They help me disconnect from the pressures of the world for a moment and appreciate the natural world around me.*

An important way to stay connected is to have a confidante. Choose someone who shares your core beliefs and is a good listener. A person you trust for good advice when you need to run something by them. Someone who won't judge you or share what you talk about with others. We have many friends we treasure, but only a few confidantes. They are priceless.

One more idea: consider contributing some time to a worthy cause. Countless charitable and ecological organizations would be thrilled to have your help. A little time here and there adds up to a real difference, and it helps you feel connected, too. It doesn't have to be big. Start with recycling — or any activity that helps the world in some small way.

Anybody seen my humanity?

Bobbi   When I teach classes to groups in my company, I always urge them to get back to basics. These days, with so much technology to choose from, it's easy to get lost in the glamorous whiz-bang and ignore the stuff that matters most.

Computers and high-tech phones are wonderful, and they've completely changed the way the world communicates. But the speed at which that communication takes place is dizzying! We're expected to have updated information at our fingertips at all times.

We receive text messages and cell phone calls from clients saying, "A For Sale sign just went up on the house across the street. What's the price?" Clients expect you to have the Multiple Listing Service streaming on your BlackBerry so not a nanosecond goes by without your full attention being focused on the real estate market. It's daunting.

We have to remind ourselves that instant information can't be confused with the basics of selling real estate. Returning to basics means going back to the human place at a human pace. This is, after all, a people profession. When you want to boost your business, go back to the simple things that work. Personal touch notes and phone calls, open houses, networking with your colleagues and friends.

Speaking of networking, we can't stress enough how important it is to maintain good relationships with your colleagues. Sometimes you have to suck it up and swallow your pride to find a solution that preserves these relationships. So many times, they've helped both of us get the inside edge on a transaction.

Agents prefer to work with someone who's known as a facilitator, not an egotistical combatant. Trust between agents is earned over time, and one "gotcha" can destroy years of goodwill. Go out of your way to help the agent on the other side of a transaction, but if you get "played," remind them not to mistake your kindness for weakness. Use the FFF approach – Friendly, Fair, Firm.

Don't second that emotion

"It's not the situation, but whether we react (negative) or respond (positive) to the situation that's important."

– Zig Ziglar

The business of sales is personal. In real estate, the product is a home — a person's nest, the heart of the family. Buying a home isn't simply a matter of logical selection followed by financial investment. It involves every member of the family and resonates far beyond the transaction.

Buying or selling a house is an emotional experience. Tiny issues can be blown way out of proportion because people feel out of control and find themselves in unfamiliar territory. Issues Realtors® see every day can seem daunting to buyers and sellers. Keeping a cool head and a warm heart helps soften and manage the impact of these situations.

Bobbi *If you're in this profession long enough, you'll get a phone call from an irate client. Something has happened or hasn't happened according to plan and the client is hopping* *mad. I've found if I let them vent without interrupting, the storm blows over by itself. I acknowledge their frustration, offer my help, and move on.*

The trick is to isolate the issues and work jointly to resolve them so things can go forward in a positive way. Most problems are solvable if you break them down into manageable bits. You simply have to refuse to be defensive or lay blame on others. It's not personal, it's simply a challenge that's arisen and has to be addressed to achieve the desired outcome. Sometimes clients just need to feel like they're contributing to the process and have done their due diligence. And sometimes they just need reassurance that they've made a good decision. A single manageable problem isn't a signal to overreact and blow a good deal.

A home sale is seldom just financially driven. Sellers leave their homes for a variety of reasons: a job relocation, a life-changing event, a sudden financial hardship, the need for more room, the desire to downsize, and so on. The common thread is change, and change is always unsettling. Often, different members of the household view the sale differently. One may embrace moving on; another may resist and resent it. Managing the transaction while recognizing the undercurrents is essential to firmly and gently guide the process along.

Occasionally, you'll give your all to a client and yet it still backfires. You may be seeing green lights all the way and find yourself suddenly blindsided. If you're a real estate agent, you know exactly what I mean. It's that blow to your gut when your buyer happens to walk into an open house, buys it on the spot without you, then calls to tell you the good news. Or the home sellers you've been helping to prepare their home for sale announce that their nephew just got his real estate license, so of course you'll understand that he'll be listing their house. It goes on and on.

Even though it hurts, you must once again take the high road and wish them well. Never forget there's always more to the story. If a situation ends up in someone else's favor, it may just boomerang back to you. If it doesn't, another will come along. We realize that this is easier said than done; we still struggle with this from time to time. No matter how strong you become, it still hurts.

The perspective of time can work in your favor. Sometimes your clients don't fully appreciate your value until they go through a transaction without you. Then you'll hear, "In retrospect, my nephew meant well, but our experience wasn't as smooth as we'd hoped." Or, "Looking back, no one was really representing us when we bought that open house." If you do the right thing, you'll get your share of the business. If you do the remarkable thing, you'll have an abundance of business.

Sticking to the summit

"Nothing focuses the mind better than the constant sight of a competitor who wants to wipe you off the map."

–Wayne Calloway

Now that you're on your game, how do you stay there? First, ask yourself if you can stretch even further. we bet you can. Here are some thoughts to consider.

- Remain in "curious mode." Stay open to new ideas, fresh approaches and innovative techniques. Strive to reinvent yourself to stay current while keeping your hard-earned experience in the mix.

- Check your enthusiasm level. Are you still excited about what you're doing? If not, how can you reignite your fire?

- Don't allow yourself to bask in your glory and become complacent with the business you have. Use the very real threat of your competition to keep you fresh and vital. Remember, people see your success and want it. That often means taking it away from you. Let your competition keep you humble and on your toes.

- Share your knowledge and experience. Become a mentor, offer to speak on topics you know well, write a column for your local newspaper. Have coffee with new arrivals and help them grow. Offer appropriate information freely when colleagues ask. Don't hoard it for fear of giving away secrets. Knowledge isn't power. The use of it is. (What if Einstein had kept the theory of relativity to himself?) When you give of yourself, you get much more in return. If you teach someone something of value, you've made an investment in his future. If you're really good — and lucky — you may even have inspired him. This ushers in the best of all possibilities: leaving a legacy. What could be better than that?

Letting go: what a concept!

The time to relax is when you don't have time for it.

— *Sydney J. Harris*

It can take ten or fifteen years in the business to understand that as long as you do your very best (that is, everything you committed to doing), you can relax. Yes, escrows are fraught with problems. Some listings just don't sell. But it does no good for the one person your clients look to for guidance to be a stressed-out mess.

What you come to recognize after some years is: You are not the principal. You are simply the agent for the principal. When you wake up to that fact, your life will change dramatically. The problems still exist, but instead of owning them, you merely lay out solutions and/or alternatives to your clients (the principals).

"Here is what we've done to generate an offer on your home. Here's your competition and the comparable homes that have sold recently. We haven't attracted any serious prospects.

Let's discuss what we need to do to attract a ready, willing, and able buyer."

This sends a very clear message: "We are in this together. I am your partner, and I will see it through. But it's your home, and your decision to adjust price, offer incentives, and so on." Suggest solutions, but remember the ultimate decision is theirs. When they set the price too high based on the data you've shared, they'll suffer the frustration of watching their home going stale on the market. On the other hand, if the home sells in its first few days on the market, they can celebrate the wise decision they made based on the current information you provided — and you can congratulate them on doing such a great job of pricing their home.

When an escrow reaches the inevitable rocky point, offer the same solution-oriented counseling. "Your buyer chose an excellent loan program. In fact, it's the best loan available, as reflected in the number of people who applied for it. The process is on overload, and the loan won't fund as quickly as we'd hoped, so we won't be able to close on time." Offer a few ideas to make the best of the situation, and encourage their thoughts, too: "Let's discuss all our options before we make a move."

By making it clear that everyone has done all they can do without placing any blame, it just becomes another business conversation instead of a highly charged exchange.

Make the difficult calls to your clients as soon as you know there are problems. It's natural to try to solve problems on your own, but it's unnecessarily stressful. Realize it isn't your problem. It's a problem, but keep it businesslike, drama-free, and solution-oriented. Your clients are allowed to indulge in a little drama, but you don't have that luxury. It's too exhausting.

Stay in close communication, but detach yourself from the dilemma. It's vital that your clients know you care and you're not abandoning them. They will very much appreciate your leadership and your sane, comforting approach. It goes a long way toward relieving their anxiety and tension, and de-stressing your life.

Feel the burnout

"The cure for boredom is curiosity. There is no cure for curiosity."

– Dorothy Parker

Remember when you first joined the ranks of the entrepreneurs? You were completely confident, possibly cocky. You drove the veterans crazy with your eternal optimism. Let's face it – the honeymoon period is an amazing time. You were excited and up for the challenge. You were living on your love of the job, and you were tireless, determined, unstoppable. You took charge of your life, and it felt great.

But that was then, and this is now. Looking back, you realize you were a little (maybe more than a little) naïve about what it takes to make it long term in the entrepreneurial world.

As you build your business, you develop a sense of accomplishment and commitment to the cause. Despite the ups and downs (you don't acknowledge the downs), eventually you reach full capacity. You're at the top of your game, equal to the task. You're not yet bored with the same old daily challenge that, by the way, is getting less challenging every day.

You start to shake it up a bit just to get that old feeling back. You stop doing what's always worked for you and try on something new and different. Well, why not? It's your business, and you're an entrepreneurial spirit. When that doesn't put the gild back on the lily, you try something else. Where exactly did that wonderfully gratifying feeling go? Why can't you get it back?

Sometimes your creativity pays off. Your new approach may even exceed your expectations. Now you must brace for the letdown. Waking up every day ready to fight and win is an amazing feeling. Once you've won, you're saddled with the deflating question, is that all there is? Every day? From now on? What will you do to feed your addiction to creativity and challenge?

Over the years we've watched far too many talented individuals enjoy stellar career success only to crash and burn as soon as they achieved their personal pinnacle of achievement. We never understood why that success didn't translate into a lifelong successful business instead of a short stopover between careers.

Lack of challenge is the main cause of burnout in entrepreneurs. Don't confuse burnout with stress. Stress arises from facing challenges that are beyond your level of competence. Burnout feels like, "been there, done that." When the highs are gone, dissatisfaction sets in, and you no longer strive for success. The solution is to learn how to infuse challenge into all areas of your life.

Once people lose themselves in their businesses, they become one-dimensional and boring to others and themselves. Step back and do a little planning and goal-setting. Take a vacation, or at least schedule regular play days. Revisit the old you and what made you happy. Take on a new hobby. Reinvent yourself.

There's a whole wide world to live in, and it's yours for the taking. Involve yourself, contribute, make a difference, give back. When you have interests outside of business, you are happier and more interesting to others. When you're happy, you attract people to you. So find a way to get happy and keep your career in its place. You certainly worked hard to get it to this level. The only stimulant you need to avoid burnout is you.

The joke's on us

Over the years, we've amassed some funny stories. Many of them arose from silly mistakes. All came with lessons only experience can teach.

The sitting son

Bobbi *When I entered real estate, I was a single mom with a young boy. There were times when I had to take him with me to evening appointments because I couldn't afford a sitter. He had a backpack full of "quiet" toys to keep him busy while I conducted business. He knew he had to stay utterly quiet and self-entertained until it was time to go.*

Happy Musings
by Sally Huss

Look forward, laugh
a lot and help others
do the same.

At the end of one such appointment, I gathered him up to leave. As we walked to the car, I noticed he was whimpering, and asked what was wrong. "Their kid bit me," he said. "I couldn't say anything, because I had to stay quiet." I felt terrible I'd put my son in a position where he couldn't come to me for help. And I was mad at the kid for biting my son. I revised the ground rules after that. I also had a good talk with the sellers. Their child apologized, and I eventually sold their house.

Roll up your sleeves

Bobbi *Remember that scene in American Beauty where Annette Bening's character arrives to host an open house and realizes the place is not presentable? That was deja vu for me. Yes, dedicated real estate agents really do pitch in and make beds, put dishes and laundry away and tidy up when we're blindsided by an open house that's not quite ready for its closeup. I have picked up dog business, hidden boudoir photos in the closet, and called my gardener with a 911. As in any business, you do what you have to do to make the most of an opportunity.*

Feline follies

Bobbi *The owner of a house I sold was preparing to move into her new home. She told me she thought it would be a good idea to have her cat spayed during the move, but just couldn't find the time to take it to the vet. She knew I liked cats, and asked if I wouldn't mind delivering Fluffy for her. So, Fluffy and I went off to the vet.*

A few days later, I went to pick up the cat and take it to its new home. When I arrived, I was horrified to see its front paws were bandaged. I just stood there dumbfounded. What was I going to say to my client? All I could spit out was, "Oh no! The cat was supposed to be spayed, not declawed!" The vet explained that my client had called and requested this procedure since Fluffy was already there. One of my nine lives disappeared that day. I've learned to draw the line on some requests.

Quick, borrow a kayak!

Bobbi I listed a house for sale one morning, and the owners immediately left on vacation. Later that afternoon, I came by to install the sign and lockbox. When I opened the front door to arrange the property brochures on the table, I mused to myself, "Wow, I don't remember the entry flooring being so shiny!" When I stepped inside, my shoes were engulfed with water. As I went further, I found myself ankle-deep. As I frantically searched for the source, I dialed my husband, who was on his way home from work. He arrived a few minutes later with a Shop-Vac and a set of tools.

He quickly pinpointed the problem: the icemaker supply line on the refrigerator had burst. Amazing how a broken icemaker line can flood an entire first floor in just a few hours. Water had soaked the carpeting and was working its way up the furniture, walls and cabinetry. I called an emergency water damage company and begged them to come out immediately. Then I made the difficult call: I had to let the vacationing owners know their home was flooded. By the time they got my message, we were well into moving furniture and pumping water. We were there until 2 a.m.

The sellers were understandably upset, but grateful I'd been there to discover the problem and limit the damage. The complete restoration took about twelve months. The owners saw it as a sign that they weren't meant to move, and they're living there still. While I lost the chance to sell this house, their word-of of-mouth goodwill has been priceless, and I have a client for life.

The mystery of the missing hearth

Martha *I once sold a house to buyers who expressed amazement that there wasn't a fireplace in the family room. After all, this was California. Didn't every home have one? When we went for the final walk-through, they were shocked and dismayed to find the sellers had removed the drapes, which had clearly been included in the sales price. But they were even more stunned to discover the sellers had also taken their bookcase, revealing – you got it – a fireplace! I asked them if they'd agree to trade the drapes for it, and you guessed it – problem solved.*

(Not) seeing the light

Bobbi *Over the years, I've made a couple of "investments" I didn't expect to make during real estate transactions. They were usually the result of tossing off a casual remark, not clearly setting expectations, or just plain being blindsided. One of my favorite ... yet somewhat painful ... examples involves a chandelier.*

I sold a house whose dining room chandelier had been a wedding present from the owner's mother. It was disclosed during the transaction that the fixture would be replaced with "like kind" before closing. When I accompanied the buyers on their final walkthrough, we discovered the sellers had indeed taken the chandelier, but had failed to replace it.

Rather than escalate what was already a tense situation, I agreed to replace it myself. I went to an upscale lighting store, purchased a chandelier that closely resembled the original, and had it installed before close of escrow. When the new owners moved in, they were outraged over the "cheap" chandelier I'd chosen. It certainly was not cheap, and it looked very much like the old one. They finally decided it would do.

Fast forward some years later, when this couple sold the home. As I previewed the property, I smiled when I noticed they'd taken the chandelier with them — and hadn't replaced it. I guess they liked it after all.

Happiness: it's in the balance

"Many people seem to think that success in one area can compensate for failure in other areas. But can it really?... True effectiveness requires balance."

–Stephen Covey

Martha *Many years ago, I wrapped my entire existence around my husband and young son. They were the center of my universe. As it should be, right? Not necessarily. This became crystal clear to me when my very young niece, Bette, visited one day and asked innocently, "But Auntie Martha, what do you do for yourself?" I was surprised, and*

Happy Musings
by Sally Huss
The slower we go, the more we observe and the more we enjoy. Pace yourself.

probably a bit defensive. But she started me thinking, and I had to admit she had a point.

Not only was my family the center of my universe, it had become the whole thing. Not necessarily the worst thing in the world, but I'd given up all of myself to create it. What was left of me? What a bore I must have become! It took a lot of thought and planning, but I was able to identify subjects, projects, and events that made me happy and more fulfilled. These interests in no way diminished my role as wife and mother. In fact, they made me much more interesting and desirable. They also made that role more fun and rewarding.

One of my decisions was to take on a part-time job. It had to be something that would allow me to stay home with Cole and help me grow. I became a Mary Kay Consultant and eventually Director of Sales. It was my inauguration into selling, and offered some of the best training I've ever received.

Mary Kay stressed that we keep our priorities straight. She advocated God first, family second, business third. Much attention was given to making your family a part of your business and making them feel special, not abandoned, when you went to work. Husbands were consulted, and their support was a large part of the women's success. If you have the full backing of your loved ones behind you, it's almost impossible to fail. I'm thankful for all I learned at that company, and I continue to draw on the wisdom Mary Kay Ash shared with her faithful followers.

In those days, I worked on three areas of my life every day. I felt if I did something for my family, something for my business, and something for myself (no matter how small), I would enjoy a lovely, full life. That formula is still the framework of my day, but I've stepped it up a bit.

Over the years I've identified areas of my life that need attention. My creative side needs to be fed regularly, as does my thirst for knowledge, travel, relationships, gardening, entertainment, — oh yes, and business.

Give some thought to what made you happy as a child. It is most likely what would make you happy today. Feed those childhood delights. You deserve them, and everyone around you will benefit from the joy you exude. You'll be more attractive to clients looking for confidence and leadership. If you can manage your life, you can certainly make a difference in theirs!

Once you've assembled the ingredients for a full and happy life, plan your days around it. Your business/life plan must reflect your interests and priorities to be effective. You owe it to yourself and everyone who loves you to live the happiest life you can imagine. Craft it today and live it every day. You can have it all.

Take responsibility — it's your life

"Maybe you don't like your job, maybe you didn't get enough sleep, well nobody likes their job, nobody got enough sleep. Maybe you just had the worst day of your life, but you know, there's no escape, there's no excuse, so just suck it up and be nice."

— Ani Difranco

Martha *Many years ago, I found myself in a shocking situation. I lost my home, and was forced to file bankruptcy. It was the most humiliating experience of my life, and I can't blame anyone but myself.*

In the early 1980s, loans — if available at all — charged record high interest rates. It was common for the seller to act as the bank to facilitate the sale. In our case, we were short just a small amount, so the seller agreed to carry an $11,000 second trust deed, due and payable several years later.

When the note came due, we didn't have the funds to pay it off. The foreclosure process began. We were told it would take 111 days. That seemed like more than enough time to find a solution. As it turns out, time passes quickly. Oh, so quickly. I trusted someone who told me everything was fine and the "problem" was taken care of. I didn't question how it had been solved. Shame on me.

Finally, a note was posted on my front door, and it was over. I vowed from that moment on I would take full responsibility for my life and never rely on anyone else again.

Everyone experiences hard times at some time point in life. No one is exempt. The only answer is to take ownership of the situation and figure out a solution to the problem. It sounds too simple, but it's what we must do to lead a healthy, fulfilled life.

There was a time when I allowed myself to get caught in the vicious cycle of emotional abuse. "I'm not good enough to do it on my own. I'll try to be a better person." Thinking back, I ask myself, "How did I let this happen?"

The truth is, these situations develop so slowly and surely, we never see them coming. We find ourselves in a relationship with a partner, boss, spouse, or anyone in a position of power, who begins to drip little negatives on us. The flow can be imperceptible at first, but it inevitably gains speed. Before you know it, you don't even have enough confidence left to set yourself free. It's a terrible position to be in. If you realize you've allowed your self-esteem to be eroded, get help. If you can't extricate yourself, call friends or get professional help to rebuild your confidence.

These are extremely tough lessons, but valuable ones. Too many people go through life finding fault and placing blame. "I didn't deserve that ticket." "My ex caused my problems." "I can't catch a break."

We make our own breaks, and we make our own luck. Mistakes will be made, and we will learn from them and grow. I am a firm believer in "packing my own chute." Take responsibility for everything you do, including what you delegate to others. The responsibility begins and ends with you.

The tipping point

"Yesterday ended last night. Every day is a new beginning. Learn the skill of forgetting and moving on."

— Norman Vincent Peale

Bobbi *Everybody has a bad day, and I had a doozy yesterday. It seemed as if I just couldn't get out of my own way — everything I touched went sideways. An escrow blew up, my clients were cranky, and I was developing a nasty headache. To top it off, I had a dentist appointment to replace an old crown at the end of the day. Even conversations with my friends seemed "off." I wanted to crawl under the covers and wait for the day to be over.*

In our business, the clients we work with are making life-changing decisions. They rely on us for guidance. It's crucial to recognize the importance of this responsibility and conduct ourselves with unwavering stability and objectivity to help them make the best possible decisions for themselves and their families.

In the process, we're privy to intimate details about their private and financial lives. Selling homes is a deeply personal profession. It's easy to fall into the trap of internalizing other people's problems and take them on as your own. Yet in order to give our clients the service they hired us to provide, we have to maintain a professional distance, compartmentalize our emotions, and resist absorbing their issues to such a point that we lose our objectivity.

Knowing all of this comes with the territory and is well and good until the day you aren't feeling up to par and one little disappointment becomes your tipping point, releasing mountains of pent-up emotion. That's when it's time to recognize you need to let it pass and reboot.

Bobbi *For me, a little exercise and a good night's sleep helps a lot. (Okay, and maybe a piece of chocolate cake).*

Next time you're hit with the blues, unless something is seriously wrong, take some comfort in knowing it happens to everyone, and it will pass.

5   A new course, and how to chart it

Having it all — your way

We often make the mistake of measuring our own success against the achievement of others. Everyone has a different definition of success. One person may define it as being number one in the company/brand/world, while the next person sees it as meeting bills on a monthly basis. Either way, we must determine what our personal success threshold is, and formulate a plan to get us there.

One excellent measure of success is earning the same amount of money year after year, but doing it in a progressively

Happy Musings
by Sally Huss
Goals get you where
you want to go, as long
as they go hand in hand
with action.

shorter period of time with less effort. What a great life you could live! Imagine: net $XXX the first year by working six days a week, eight hours a day. The next year, trim costs and put systems in place that net the same $XXX in five days, working only six hours a day. Fine-tune this system over time, and you could master the four-hour work week, leaving the remainder of your life to simply live!

Programming your personal GPS

"All you have to do is know where you're going. The answers will come to you of their own accord."

— Earl Nightingale

No one would argue the importance of knowing where you're going. In fact, it takes goals to create a business and/or life plan at all. You work backward to determine what level of financial success you need to reach them, as well as fund your investments and retirement.

Happy Musings
by Sally Huss

It is always the blindness to our weaknesses that do us in. The better we see, the better we do.

Martha *Over the years, I set my business goals in relation to dollars earned and units sold. In the late 1980s, I used my new computer skills to make a chart with cute little icons in the shape of houses and blanks for the addresses of homes I'd sold and the date that I'd sold them. My goal for that particular year was to sell three homes a month. I started in January. I was very proud of my chart, which hung on the wall next to my desk for all the world to see. By March, I was ahead of the game with ten homes sold. Unfortunately, I failed to factor in my lack of control of the marketplace. In April, the market died. By June, I was devastated and feeling like a loser. Falling short was wreaking havoc with my confidence level. Nothing good had come from setting goals over which I had no control.*

Action goals are the answer. Set action goals, rather than dollar goals, and you actually have the power to meet them. Revisit every mode of prospecting that's been successful for you in the past. Set goals like knocking on just ten doors a day. Regardless of the weather or what shoes you're wearing, you can manage to knock on at least ten doors. Write five note cards a day to past clients and your sphere of influence. Once again, no matter how busy you are or what stands in the way, you can manage five note cards. Then top it off with a resolution to hold one open house a weekend, and you have a winning recipe.

We promise if you knock on ten doors a day, write five note cards, and hold one open house per weekend, you will generate sales. Add on more and bigger prospecting activities for more and bigger goals. They might not come in the time frame you expect, but if you take action on a consistent basis, the sales will follow — year after year.

A number of real estate gurus talk about how they earned amazing total commissions in a single year. However, if you break it down to see what's left after paying for their team of assistants and the expensive marketing programs it takes to generate those numbers, the figure becomes much less exciting.

It's all about the bottom line. Think in terms of what you keep, not what you make.

Take some time to revisit your marketing plan at the beginning of the year and regularly throughout the year. What's working and what isn't? Weigh the results of each program, and make any needed adjustments right away. If one technique is profitable, step it up. If something hasn't paid off, don't throw good money after bad.

Even top agents have been guilty of farming an area far too long with no measurable results. We justify this behavior by telling ourselves we're just about to have a breakthrough. Honestly evaluate the situation. Could that money be better spent by stepping up a program that's working to make it work even better?

Don't panic, it's just a goal

What is it about setting goals that scares us so? You'd think we'd be automatically wired to know where we want to go and how we're going to get there. Sometimes we're "poisoned by possibilities." Too many choices.

Sometimes, we compare ourselves to other people who actually want different things out of life than we do, and we feel intimidated, confused, and stuck. The first step in erasing the trepidation is making sure your goals are truly your goals and not someone else's.

Begin by giving serious thought to who you are and what you want out of life. Some people are driven by competition, pulling out all the stops to be Number One in their fields. Others simply want to have a quiet life and live within their means. Both can be very successful. Everyone has a different definition of success.

Next, make sure that your goals are aligned. Immersing yourself in parenting while your children are young — helping regularly in the classroom, coaching their sports teams — is an admirable goal. But it should not be in place the same year you decide to break all sales records in your office. When you set incompatible goals, you set yourself up for frustration and defeat. You simply can't reach a goal that requires spending time in the classroom and on the soccer field at the same time you've resolved to be in front of as many clients as possible.

For a new beginning, just begin

Success is the progressive realization of a worthy goal.

Know what the very best thing about today is? You can start fresh, begin a new pattern of positive results, one simple step at a time. This could be the moment your life changes for the better — forever! The key? Just begin.

Let's be honest

How would you rate yourself on the following? (Be truthful, no one's looking.) Would you say you're getting better or worse in the following categories?

- Your health

- Your attitude

- Your relationships

- Your finances

- Your career

- Your contribution (what you're giving back)

Consider the answers. Set a few goals in response. Then start taking small, positive steps on a consistent basis until your meet them. In other words, just begin. Step off the cliff. Have faith. The results are in the future, but the little positive things you need to do must be done today and every day. Even though you can't see the results right now, or tomorrow, or the next day, you must have unshakable faith that they will appear. One tiny step, one positive choice at a time, every time, every day. You may not feel like doing the thing you need to do today. Do it anyway and make it a habit.

Someday doesn't exist

Only today, this very moment, exists. We all know bad things happen that are simply out of our control. We experience setbacks, failures and inexplicable bad luck. What separates the winners from the losers is how we react. You can't change the past, but you can impact the future. In fact, you will impact the future, either positively or negatively; there is no neutral. You are either getting better or getting worse. It's your choice.

Don't get busy, get productive

What actions will you take today to contribute to your success? A few examples to spark your thought process:

- Write a note to someone you were thinking about

- Read a few pages of good self-development book

- Eat an apple instead of a bag of potato chips

- Pass on your daily latte to save $3.50

- Take a brisk walk before or after work instead of turning on the TV

Being productive vs. being busy

What positive actions did you take today that contributed to your success?

What busywork could you have eliminated?

What tasks do you perform that don't need doing at all, could be done in half the time if you focused, or could be delegated to others? They say work expands to fill the allotted time, and most people leave 80% of the work to be done in the last 20% of the time. Think about how much you're able to accomplish in the hours before you leave on vacation. You become a whirling dervish of efficiency! That is focused purpose, not wasted effort.

Helpful Note: Find a mentor. The person you choose doesn't even have to know about it. Model what he or she does well; successful people leave a trail of evidence. You'll discover many have their own coaches — personal fitness coaches, life coaches, career coaches, coaches of all types. Your coach/ mentor could be the successful person in the office across the hall.

Ask tough questions

1. Where are you today, and where do you want to be tomorrow?

2. What does financial security mean to you, and what steps will you take to get there?

3. How many people do you honestly need to talk with to generate the number of clients you need to meet your sales goals?

4. How did this year's production compare to last year's?

5. Are you charging what you're worth? If not, why not?

6. On a scale of one to ten, evaluate yourself:

    - Professional knowledge: How will you stay ahead of the curve?

    - Marketing Tools: Are you using them effectively?

    - Sales skills: How will you polish and upgrade them regularly?

    - Leads and referrals: Are you effectively converting them to closed sales?

- Your public image and reputation

- Your attitude

- Your well-being

7. What are the current market conditions?

8. What changes do you anticipate in those conditions?

9. How will you adapt to those changes?

10. How would you describe yourself compared to your competition?

11. What other important factors do you see affecting your performance next year?

Need a jump-start? Try these.

1. Where do your clients come from? "How did you happen to call me today?"

2. How successful are your marketing campaigns? Is it money well spent? In other words, did you generate results?

3. What new, different, innovative or simply "tried and true" tool can you implement to boost business? (Take cues from someone else's successful campaign.)

4. What areas of your business need improving? (Take classes, read books, listen to CD's, work with a mentor.)

5. What steps can you take to bring more balance to your life?

6. Are you monitoring your time? Are you making the highest and best use of it?

7. Do you have effective systems in place?

8. Are you organized? Keeping to your schedule? Writing things down?

9. Are you ready for success? Are you willing to accept the consequences of not achieving your goals?

Goal-setting in six easy steps

These guidelines work in all areas of your life, from career to parenting to spiritual development.

1. Goals must be your own, not someone else's.

2. Goals must be written, specific and achievable — and have a defined deadline.

3. Keep your goals in front of you — literally. Read them every day. Create a Vision Board with pictures of your goals, and put it where you'll see it every day.

4. Be willing to make the commitment to your goals and sacrifice to achieve them.

5. Make a plan. Not a "set in stone" plan, just a plan. Think of it as your starting point. Baby steps. It will change and morph into another plan, followed by another as you develop and grow.

6. Do something positive every day. Think about bad habits you'll replace with good habits. Choose one. Start small.

Your daily choices are a result of your habits of thought. Your view of the world and how you fit in it forms your basic philosophy of life. The long-term effect of your everyday habits of thought and action shape that philosophy.

Bobbi *A weird thing happened on the way to this book. I made a Vision Board at the outset of this project. I cut out pictures of career goals, health goals, recreation goals, personal goals. It is framed and hangs above my computer where I glance at it many times a day. One by one they are materializing. Try it—you will see your goals being met one by one. It feels wonderfully fulfilling, and energizes you to reach more goals.*

The vision statement and why you need it

A vision statement nails down your basic philosophy and business purpose in concrete terms. It could be about making a positive difference in the lives of the people and community you serve. Or providing the best real estate service in your marketplace. It could be about giving expert advice based upon market knowledge. Or being the best negotiator. It could encompass all these things and more.

The key to an effective vision statement is C-R-E-A-T-E.

Concise and clear. State your goals as clearly as you can.

Realistic. Believe you can and will make this happen. Keeping your goals realistic ensures success. When you achieve it, build on it one small step at a time. If you've successfully set and achieved goals in the past, expand them. When you reach that next target, stretch yourself a bit more.

Enthusiasm. Do your goals excite you? Do they inspire a passion that won't let you rest until you achieve them? If not, continue working on your vision. You will eventually tap into one that makes you leap out of bed in the morning and wish for more hours in the day.

Attitude. You must approach this process positively. State your goals as "I will…" or "I have…" Thoughts are things. You get what you ask for, so ask for and expect success.

Time. There must be a deadline. Assign a specific date for reaching your goal. Otherwise it will expand and forever be elusive. Goals are dreams that have been imagined in detail … and given a timeline.

Evidence. The results of this approach will speak for themselves.

Now CREATE your own personal vision:

Now that I've got it, what do I do with it?

Once you've created a clear vision statement, direct your unconscious mind to focus on every resource available to get you there.

Picture living the life you want. How will it feel to be in control of your finances, connected with family and friends? To spend time doing what you enjoy with people you enjoy? Do you feel confident? In control? On top of the world?

Always state your goals in positive language. "I will get out of debt" is much better than "I want to get out of debt." The first statement is positive. The second statement focuses on the debt. Your subconscious mind will move you toward your focus: debt. A completely positive goal would change the words, "getting out of debt" to "achieving financial security."

Martha *The phrase that works best for me is, "I will achieve financial serenity." I'm not sure we ever have the luxury of financial security, in view of the ups and downs of the economy. Financial serenity means you can sleep at night.*

I find that to be the most important goal when it comes to my financial well-being.

Let's visualize for a moment, and create a positive, first-person description of what complete, unqualified success and accomplishment of your goals would feel like. Design it using the system above. It should be a statement like:

It is (date) and I am _____. I see_____. I hear_____. I feel_____. I'm doing_____. I'm saying_____.

If you can see it, you can do it. Put yourself in that picture and live the moment. What do you see, feel, hear? Make it as detailed and real as you possibly can. The more defined the vision, the more your subconscious mind has to work with. Now hold onto that moment. Step back into the real world, but keep that vision in your head and your heart. You have the power to make it happen. You can shape your future – it's just a matter of formulating a plan and going to work on it.

Bobbi's breakthrough

"There is more to us than we know. If we can be made to see it, perhaps for the rest of our lives we will be unwilling to settle for less."

— *Kurt Hahn*

You'd think everyone would want to achieve as much success as possible, wouldn't you? And isn't achieving success simply a matter of deciding what it is we want to do and then doing it? So why do some people find success so elusive?

Let me tell you about the turning point when my "success ceiling" changed. In about my fifth year of selling real estate, I was enjoying some success, but I was stuck. I couldn't figure out how to get to the next level of achievement. That's when I signed up for a class called Quantum Leap. Its goal was to help people determine why they reached a plateau and could progress no further.

Through a series of exercises, I came to realize I was afraid of too much success. I was subconsciously asking myself, "Why do I deserve success? What will happen to me if I become successful? Who will I be then? What will my family think of me?" I learned that sometimes a barrier or limit is just something you put there. It doesn't really exist. I also learned that many people have trouble achieving success beyond the level reached by their parents. I was one of them.

My father was a career military man, a Navy helicopter pilot who became an air traffic controller with the FAA after he retired from the service. He was certainly successful, but not wealthy. The light bulb went off for me after my Quantum Leap experience. When the class was over, I called my dad and told him what I had just experienced. I timidly asked for his permission to take on more challenges in my career, and perhaps make more money than he did at the height of his career. He didn't hesitate for a moment — he encouraged me to go as far as I wanted to and achieve as much success as I dreamed of having. He told me he was my biggest cheerleader. Boom! I let it rip and never looked back.

After my breakthrough moment came work and dedication. I learned success comes from commitment, hard work, confidence and yes, even lots of failure. It's trite, but true. I guess I was lucky that I didn't achieve success easily; I was given plenty of learning opportunities. I learned that what worked in one situation didn't necessarily work in all. Failure teaches lessons — not fun, but necessary. The trick is applying these nuggets to the next step in reaching your goals. Learning something new takes you out of your comfort zone. You risk failing, but it gets easier over time.

It's hard to leave what's comfortable to experiment with new approaches. But if you apply new, creative solutions to existing challenges, you open the door to learning better and more effective ways of realizing your goals. When you feel uncomfortable reaching for the next level, it means you're growing and pushing through your fear of failure. And it's said that every failure brings with it the seed of equal success.

Remember Edison's light bulb? Through persistence and determination, he came up with an electric incandescent light bulb after thousands and thousands of experimental filaments failed. His invention changed the world. Your perseverance can change yours.

6 Take it higher

Giving back

"We make a living by what we get. We make a life by what we give."

—Sir Winston Churchill

You have now taken your business and your life to a new level. You have momentum. It took focused energy and unbridled enthusiasm to get you there. Now comes the tough part. How will you maintain that level now that you've achieved it? How will you keep it fresh now that the newness has worn off?

Happy Musings
by Sally Huss

Each day is a lifetime
to be lived fully, joyfully
and without regret.

©2007 Sally Huss, Dist. by King Features Syndicate

The process of building momentum in life/business is much like a speedboat on the open ocean. If you're chugging along slowly, the waves will wear you out. You'll be constantly buffeted and pushed around. It's a constant battle. As you build up speed (momentum), you skim right over the crest of the wave, bypassing all the choppiness and struggle. The question is, how does one gather enough speed and maintain enough momentum to always ride the crest?

Part of the power that keeps you there is giving back. We contribute to the community because it's the right thing to do and, let's face it, it makes us feel good. We start out working hard to make money to provide for our families and to get ahead. That's Part One. When we achieve a certain level of success and have accumulated many "things," we need to proceed to Part Two. It's time to balance life out by giving back.

The universe is very adept at keeping track of this give and take, and those who don't give back once in a while usually run into a brick wall. Pay it forward. You feel good, the recipient of your kindness feels good, and the momentum goes on. Make giving back a habit. Whatever you put out into the universe comes back tenfold, so don't be afraid to share the wealth.

Send out daily...

- Kind thoughts or kind words

- Support and encouragement

Give freely of...

- Your resources (time and money) to worthy causes

- Your ideas, insight, and knowledge

Martha *Over the years, I've always held weekly sales meetings. In the mid 1990s, I read the book Gung Ho by Ken Blanchard, and it changed the way I thought about synergy in an office environment. It's all about catching each other doing things right. Doing this helps build morale and boost enthusiasm within your organization.*

The message resonated with me, and I introduced the idea to the agents. They loved it, and I incorporated a Gung Ho experience into every meeting. It gives the agents a chance to recognize and publicly thank an associate for stepping up and lending a hand in some small way each week. The person giving the Gung Ho feels good, the recipient feels rewarded, and a wonderful feeling of respect and camaraderie permeates the office. Giving in even the smallest way makes such a difference.

Remember the Butterfly Effect — the scientific theory that a butterfly flapping its wings in South America can affect the weather in Central Park? Translate this to our species — human beings. The smallest acts of kindness can surely change the world.

Find joy… every day

"What we call the secret of happiness is no more a secret than our willingness to choose life."

– Leo Buscaglia

We've talked a lot about attaining a balanced life. But that's not enough. No matter how busy you are, you can learn to take time to smell the roses. As this book was evolving, the emails were flying fast and furiously between us. We're both usually on the same wavelength – very quick and to the point. But often, our super-charged memos were softened by delightful little asides: "Did you see the incredible sunset tonight? The sky was striped with pink and orange!" or, "I have two deer decorating my lawn…yes, real ones!"

Martha *While a balanced life is crucial to your long-term happiness, recognizing a moment of pure joy can lighten your load tremendously. When my daughter first moved away to college, I was feeling a little empty nest syndrome, to put it mildly. While reading my mail one Saturday morning, I opened a card to find a photo of a perfect dew-dropped rose with the caption, "out for a walk and wanted* *to share this with you." Two dozen long-stemmed hothouse roses could not have pleased me more than that picture.*

So many people miss joyous opportunities waiting for life's big moments. We put too much stock in these events, then feel deflated when they finally arrive. (Think about the restaurant or movie your friend raved about that you didn't think was all that great.) Little, unexpected, joyous moments add up to momentous happiness if you're open to them. But you must commit to paying them forward by smiling at a stranger, giving someone a sincere compliment, or performing some other simple, spontaneous nicety.

Think of this word — serendipity: "the effect by which one accidentally discovers something fortunate, especially while looking for something else entirely." Isn't that fun? Always be open to the moment. And remember, it's the little things.

Get comfortable with compliments

"Courtesies of a small and trivial character are the ones which strike deepest in the grateful and appreciating heart."

– Henry Clay

Practice giving compliments. It's habit-forming. Mean what you say; don't give a compliment with one breath and take it away with the next. "I like the way you're wearing your hair now" sounds very much like, "Your hair looks so much better this way than the way you used to wear it." It sounds similar, but it sure doesn't feel the same. Some people either don't know how to give a compliment, or they simply can't think of anything nice to say. Giving compliments is a lovely art, and well worth making a little effort to cultivate.

Martha *I recently came across a study showing how giving and receiving compliments affects endorphins. The giver gets a rush of them and immediately feels better. The recipient enjoys the same thing. What a wonderfully easy way to improve your day, and that of everyone you come in contact with!*

Sometimes when we see someone, we have a positive reaction — but the moment passes before we have a chance to share it. Try to revisit that thought after the fact. It's so easy to leave a very short and sweet voicemail or email message: "When I saw you earlier today, I noticed you looked wonderful in that color. We were moving so fast I didn't have a chance to tell you. Have a great rest of your day." That little bit of effort on your part goes a long way. The lucky recipient feels good about your message. You feel good for taking the time to leave it.

On the other hand, why do we feel the need to negate every compliment given to us?

"Love your dress. Is it new?"

"Oh, this old thing? I cleaned my closet and I'm recycling some old outfits."

Why do we throw away a sincere compliment? Don't fight it, simply say, "Yes, thank you!" or "No, it's not new, but thank you just the same!" A gracious thank you is all it takes to get the endorphins flowing in both directions.

Relax and enjoy the ride

"Don't forget until too late that the business of life is not business, but living."

– B.C. Forbes

As we travel though life, the significance of some experiences escapes us until much later. Isn't it interesting how events that seemed random at the time eventually make sense? Just keep "falling forward," experiencing as much as possible, participating in life as much as you can, and the interconnectedness of it all will eventually become clear.

Happy Musings
by Sally Huss

Kind words
are easily spoken.

Learn to live by this (paraphrased) line from Max Ehrmann's poem, "Desiderata": "No doubt the universe is unfolding as it should … and I'm at peace with that." Say this every time you hit a brick wall or suffer a disappointment. It will help center you. What you just experienced happened for a reason, and in time you will understand. Let yourself go with the flow of life, and everything will work out in the end.

Spend some time reflecting on the journey you've taken so far and see how perfectly it all fits together. Give some thought to what you might do to make things easier along the way ahead. Here are a few ideas to get you started:

1. Live your life by design. Meditate, take a walk, or simply spend a little quiet time and figure out what you really want. The opposite of living by design is living by default — that is, by settling. Set your goals, break them down into easy steps, and live with purpose.

2. Let go of resistance. It's a struggle. Don't you sometimes just get tired of the strain? It doesn't have to be that way. Let go and watch what happens!

3. Be prepared. When you're prepared, you can relax and enjoy life more. Preparation involves taking care of

your mind and body. Eating well and exercising. Being informed and being curious. Working on yourself and being receptive to new ideas. As you expand who you are, your sense of what is possible in your life expands, too.

4. Work together. You can't do it alone, and you really don't want to. When you are open and willing to honestly share, you create energy in your life that is greater than the sum of its parts.

5. Move out of your comfort zone. If you continue to live there, your life will forever be on hold. Unless you make some changes, you'll never experience the personal freedom that comes with putting yourself out there. Getting into the flow of life involves risk, but that's exactly what you need. When you're in the flow, your energy keeps expanding and you're always looking forward to what's next.

6. Practice an attitude of gratitude. As you reflect on the journey you've taken so far and see how all those seemingly random experiences fit together, you'll gradually begin to understand how abundant your life

really is. Be grateful for the path you have chosen, but at the same time be ready for the next step. When it comes, recognize and enjoy it.

Life is unpredictable — you don't always get to figure it out. Enjoy the adventure. Think about being a more fulfilled person who's more engaged with life every day.

Love is the answer

"Ability is what you're capable of doing. Motivation determines what you do. Attitude determines how well you do it."

– Lou Holtz

Bobbi *I love my job. This is not to say that I don't sometimes feel frustrated, tired, bored or annoyed with some part of it. I've hit some real rough patches during my career. One time I was so verbally abused by a client, I spent the night crying on my bathroom floor. That only happened once. What doesn't kill you makes you stronger!*

Real estate presents a variety of opportunities and challenges. Of course I enjoy some aspects of my job more than others. But I wake up each morning ready and eager to go to work. I've tried on a few different careers, from teaching school to selling wine to restaurants to being a real estate broker. I've loved each one. But I'm absolutely passionate about my career in real estate.

Back when I graduated from college, my gender seemed to limit my career choices. It felt like girls were preconditioned to become nurses or teachers. I didn't get the nurse gene, so I became a teacher.

While I loved the job, I had no idea I was really training for a different one, a career in sales. I explain my sales ability this way: If you can sell social studies to sixth graders at two in the afternoon when they know school is about to be let out for the day, you can sell anything.

A schoolteacher's skills are really sales skills. They include making a lesson plan for the week, one for each day, and one for each subject. Testing to see if the students grasped the concepts. Keeping good records and adapting teaching methods to a variety of learning styles and personalities.

Skilled teachers maintain control of the class while promoting a spirit of camaraderie and teamwork. They must effectively communicate and work with the kids, their parents and their colleagues. Teachers are rewarded daily with the joy of helping others achieve their goals. But their big reward is nearly a year away, when their work enables their classes to progress to the next grade. The same process, packaged in a different way, can be used to sell wine, houses or just about anything else, including ourselves. If you work at something you love, the day flies by.

If you combine passion with commitment, money follows. One of my mentors told me, "Show up on time, tell the truth, and don't get attached to the outcome." What he meant was, do your job to the best of your ability and let the rest go. The outcome may not be the one you were hoping for, but it is what it is, and you did your best.

If you bend the truth or approach a situation with only your own best interests at heart, it may work out in your favor this time, but you're setting yourself up for certain demise. The authenticity will be missing. Soon, you won't love what you do, and the downward spiral will begin.

If you don't love what you are doing now, you may simply be in training for what you were really meant to do. Take a chance. It's not too late. Take it one tiny step at a time. You can do it. Just begin.

About Martha

I was raised in a 1600-square-foot home in Norwalk, California, shoehorned in with five siblings, assorted cats and birds, and lots of stuff. It was a boisterous, haphazard Irish Catholic clan with a simple and uncomplicated life. We survived on a single income, a civil servant's salary. If we wanted to do anything extracurricular, we were allowed and encouraged, but we had to make it happen on our own. Parenting was very different in those days. Call it "hands-free" style. There was not much chance that an über-involved adult would help with homework, much less a project or a merit badge.

I was an excellent student. I attended Catholic school for eight years, then spent my high school days recovering from it. I attended college, but stopped short at an AA degree and never went back. I'm not proud of that. My family values education highly, and I should have seen it through. From time to time I think about going back and finishing, but common sense prevails and I escape without adding unnecessary stress to my life. That's one line in the sand I've decided not to cross at this late date.

My mother believed in me. She praised me, encouraged me and told me I could do anything I wanted to do. It turns out she was pretty close to right. Despite my humble beginnings, I've managed to succeed in an industry where many fail, or at best, cling by their fingernails. I'm at the top of my game. I've made more money than I ever thought possible. I'm frugal, and I've invested well in some cases, a little irresponsibly in others. In spite of my mistakes, I have slowly but surely amassed a sizable estate.

In a nutshell, I've made a good life.

Now that I've covered all that is measurable and less important, let's talk about what is immeasurable and most important.

I'm happy. I am living my best life. I'm well-rounded and well-adjusted. I live a very organized life. Organization in your mind and your world is a critical element for enjoying a balanced life. No areas of mine are empty, lacking, or chaotic. If I want something, I go to work on it. I continue to dream big. Who knows what the future will bring?

About Bobbi

We moved around a lot when I was little; my father was a Chief in the Navy. I remember going to second grade in both Florida and Northern California. I learned to make friends quickly and fit in. By the time I started third grade, we had settled into the home I'd live in until I graduated from high school.

My mother was a stay-at-home mom, volunteering at the library, serving as a Girl Scout leader, active in the PTA. My sister and I always had pets at home—dogs, cats, fish. We lived in a modest three-bedroom house my parents chose because it was walking distance from school. Our family vacations were usually to national parks with a trailer my dad pulled behind our Buick.

I was a good kid who loved to play outdoors. But when I lost track of time and came home after five p.m. (a big "no-no" in my household), I'd hear my middle name being called and I knew I was in trouble. Bobbi Joyce! Uh-oh. I'd be put on "restriction," with my privileges taken away for a period of time.

Speaking of restriction, once when I was sixteen, I drove the family car when my parents weren't home. Somehow, they found out about it (my sister swore she didn't tell), and I was put on restriction for three months — no car privileges! After I served my time, my mom wrote me a note about parents' love and their responsibility for raising trustworthy adults. I carry that note in my wallet to this day — it's tattered and fragile now, but it's one of my most treasured possessions.

I graduated from Cal State Long Beach with a degree in sociology and a Teaching Credential. I was just 21 when I graduated, and I started teaching elementary school at barely 22. On my first day of teaching, I was asked to leave the teacher's lounge; the other teachers thought I was one of the students. To add to my humiliation, I had parents coming to my classroom to watch me teach because they'd heard I was just a child myself. (At the end of the school year, those same parents asked me to teach the next grade, so their children could have me again.) It was a challenging year, but I managed to earn the respect of my colleagues and my students' parents. I remember feeling exhausted at the end of each day from having to act so mature.

Teaching school inspired me in so many ways. The most important thing I learned was that to teach, you must first learn the subject well yourself and then find a way to communicate what you know to someone else. I learned to be creative in my presentations, and most of all to find a way to make each subject relevant and fun. Being a teacher prepares you to do many things, including manage crises, expect the unexpected, and see the best in people.

When I got married and had my son, I decided I needed a bit more flexibility in my work schedule. I wanted to go into sales. I sold wine to restaurants for Gallo and another large Southern California distributor. After about six years, I decided to get my real estate license and try my luck selling big ticket items: houses! It was a natural fit for me. Real estate combines the best of all worlds, and poses some of the biggest challenges. I love that each day is different and that I'm constantly learning. There's just no time to be bored.

Now, after over twenty years as a real estate broker, I've come full circle to become a teacher again. I want to teach a little of what I've learned to you. I hope you'll find something here that resonates with you and makes your day a little brighter.

7   Appendix: Doing the math

How to set your annual income goal for next year

1. Divide your income goal amount by 12 to establish your monthly goal.

2. Divide your monthly goal by the average commission you earned per transaction last year. This is the number of homes you must sell each month to achieve your goal.

Does this year's commission goal exceed last year's? Does it exceed the amount of last year's earned income?

Example: A target annual commission of $150,000 divided by 12 equals $12,500 per month. If your past average commission earned per transaction was $6,500, you can reach your goal by selling two houses a month. (Adjust up or down depending upon the average sales price in your marketplace.)

Remember, some months you'll sell more than your goal amount, and some months you may fall short. If you keep aiming at your goal and committing to the process, you'll hit your target at the end of the year.

Not so fast – you also need an annual sales objective

Since not all listings sell, your listing inventory must be greater than the number of sold listings you need to meet your goal. Market conditions will also impact this figure.

By the way, remember markets fluctuate. Sometimes they favor sellers, other times buyers. It isn't wise to put all your eggs in one basket – build expertise in all aspects of your business.

Got more goals?

Do you want to be a stronger listing agent, capture greater market share in a territory, be top agent in your office, buy a new car or home, enjoy a great vacation? Describe each goal in detail.

Contract with myself

I will prospect ("touch" potential clients) a total of ___ hours per week. To do this:

- I will host a minimum of __ open houses per month.

- I will mail/walk-drop/email ___ just listed or just sold cards to my farm area each month. (Other "touch" opportunities could include promotional materials such as notepads, market updates, calendars and the like, used as mailers or handouts.)

Happy Musings
by Sally Huss

Got a goal? Without
a doubt you will succeed.
With a doubt you might not.

©2008 Sally Huss. Dist. by King Features Syndicate. www.SallyHuss.com

- I will write (by hand!) and mail (first class postage!) __ personal notes to my sphere of influence/past clients each week.

- I will host client appreciation events.

- I will send email blasts containing relevant real estate information.

- I will network within my areas of interest. (If you are a tennis player, play tennis!)

- I will send regular newsletters.

- I will focus on working (without being distracted by interruptions) ___ hours per day.

- I will set aside a budget of ___% of my projected annual income for marketing and personal development tools.

- I will contribute ___% of my monthly income to my savings plan.

- I will contribute in the following ways to my...

  Family:

  Health:

  Happiness:

  Community:

- I will review my goals daily, track my performance, and review my plan to make adjustments as I grow and develop my business.

Weekly Tracking Guide

The key to goal realization is small-bite management. Track how many times each day you perform the following to reach your weekly goals:

	Monday	Tuesday	Wednesday
Number of client contacts			
Leads generated			
Appointments taken			
Followup actions taken			
Marketing pieces			
Family obligations			
Exercise			
Personal time			

Thursday	Friday	Saturday	Sunday	Totals

If you commit to this, the money will follow.

Once you've set annual goals, the next step is long-range thinking. What will your life look like five years from now? How will you get there?

Choose Success: Plan, Do, Review

My plan for success is:

My Goals

1.   Next Year's Goal for Annual Income:

2.   Next Year's Goal for Units Sold:

3.   Next Year's Personal Goals: